THE KUNDALINI EXPERIENCE

THE KUNDALINI EXPERIENCE

PSYCHOSIS OR TRANSCENDENCE?

Lee Sannella, M.D.

INTEGRAL PUBLISHING
1992

A revised and expanded edition of *Kundalini: Psychosis or Transcendence?*
published by H. S. Dakin Company. © 1976 by Lee Sannella

Printed in the United States of America.

Published by Integral Publishing
P.O. Box 1030
Lower Lake, California 95457

To my father, Salvatore Sannella,
who practiced medicine until his ninetieth year

Cover illustration by Experimental Design, Ltd., Kent, Ohio.

*Grateful acknowledgment is made to the Dawn Horse Press for permission to quote
from the works of Da Love-Ananda.*

Library of Congress Catalog Card Number: 87-080679
ISBN 0-941255-28-X (hardcover)
ISBN 0-941255-29-8 (paperback)

Printing (last digit) 9 8 7 6

CONTENTS

PREFACE

Tissue is torn, blood vessels are severed, blood is spilled, and much fluid is lost; the heart races and the blood pressure soars. There is moaning, crying, and screaming. A severe injury? No, only a relatively normal human birth. The description sounds pathological because the symptoms were not discussed in relation to the outcome: a new human being.

In a darkened room a man sits alone. His body is swept by muscle spasms. Indescribable sensations and sharp pains run from his feet up his legs and over his back and neck. His skull feels as if it is about to burst. Inside his head he hears roaring sounds and high-pitched whistling. His hands burn. He feels his body tearing within. Then suddenly he laughs and is overcome with bliss.

A psychotic episode? No, this is a psychophysiological trans-formation, a "rebirth" process as natural as physical birth. It seems pathological only because the symptoms are not understood in relation to the outcome: a psychically transformed human being.

When allowed to progress to completion, this process may culminate in deep psychological balance, inner strength, and emotional maturity. Its initial stages, however, often share the violence, helplessness, and imbalance that attend the start of extra-uterine human life.

For thousands of years this transformative process has been hinted at, often only in veiled terms. Earliest references to it can be found in the most ancient scriptures of India, the Vedas. This archaic knowledge formed the basis for the later esoteric teachings as expounded in the Upanishads, Agamas, Tantras, and Samhitas, and especially the many texts belonging to the Hatha Yoga tradition.

But knowledge of this "rebirth" process was by no means

confined to India. It was an integral part of the esoteric teachings of Tibetan Buddhism, Chinese Taoism, the spirituality of certain American Indian tribes, and, as we shall see, even of the Bushmen of Africa. According to E. A. S. Butterworth (1970), there is evidence that knowledge of this transmutative process actually existed in the ancient Sumerian civilization. But we need not necessarily assume that it was diffused from there. As Jean Gebser (1985), Erich Neumann (1970), Ken Wilber (1981), and others have suggested, early humanity was rather strongly predisposed to psychic experiences, as are indeed many non-Western peoples.

It was, however, in Hindu India that the process was most carefully studied and conceptually elaborated. There it became known as *kundalini-bodhana* or the "awakening of the kundalini." The Sanskrit word *kundalini* means literally "she who is coiled," which is a picturesque metaphor for the serpent. I shall explain later the ramifications of meaning surrounding this esoteric concept and phenomenon. Suffice it to say here that the *kundalini* or, as it is also frequently referred to, the *kundalini-shakti* or "serpent power," is conceived as a form of psychospiritual energy. It is the "energy of consciousness."

What this means will be made clear in this book, inasmuch as it can be communicated in words. Those who are adept at the kundalini process characteristically emphasize that the kundalini can only be truly understood through firsthand experience.

The process of psychophysiological transformation was, until recently, apparently confined to distant cultures, esoteric traditions, and a handful of isolated individuals. Accounts of it have, as a rule, been in highly personal terms, often permeated with vague mysticism and strange mythology. As a result, the descriptions were not taken seriously by Western students of the human psyche. This, in turn, delayed the systematic comparison of available materials from different traditions, which would have shown that the kundalini process is an important phenomenon that deserves most careful attention from scientists. Thus, for a long time, those few professionals who encountered this phenomenon could feel justified in taking a skeptical and suspicious stance toward it.

In the 1970s two significant developments occurred that

changed this situation sufficiently to challenge the prevalent pro-fessional mind-set. The first development was the marked increase in the number of people undergoing intense psychospiritual experi-ences within our own culture (see Greeley and McCready 1975). And the second was that, after a decades-long taboo on conscious-ness, Western scientists began to consider consciousness a viable subject for research again. This led to studies on the *objective* aspects of those processes that had hitherto been addressed only in esoteric or symbolic terms and that had consequently eluded the inquiries of Western science.

Today it is possible to compare the psychospiritual experiences of different traditions by applying a uniform set of standards, as well as to employ the same standards in a clinical context.

There is indeed a remarkable uniformity in the descriptions of the transformative process from widely disparate traditions. This is also the point of view of Gopi Krishna (1971), whose writings have been instrumental in popularizing the kundalini process in the West. He argued that the recorded experiences of Christian mystics, Sufi masters, and Yoga adepts make it obvious that the fundamental features of the psychophysiological transformation are the same. A study of the various traditional accounts for which enough detail is recorded reveals symptom patterns and experiential phenomena that are strikingly similar to those found in the clinical cases cited in this book.

I will argue that these common aspects have physiological components, and that activation of a single physiological mechanism is at the root of the wide diversity of kundalini phenomena we encounter. If these two assumptions are correct, the idea of psychophysiological transmutation can no longer be considered a confusing jumble of primitive superstition, religious dogma, and wild rumor. Rather, we must begin to look again, and more seriously, at much of what scientism has tried to debunk as meaningless and worthless fantasy. In fact, we must embark on a new type of "demythologizing," namely the demythologizing of the myths of scientific materialism.

Granting, as I feel we must, that the kundalini phenomenon is real and of great significance, we can now pose several questions:

How is this phenomenon best understood? What are its basic features? How does it unfold? What is its optimal form? Does it really lead, as is widely claimed, to the appearance of psychic powers? How does the transformative process differ from normality, on the one hand, and from psychosis, on the other? Is it merely another "altered" state of consciousness, or is it something more?

I begin by considering the last question first. The kundalini process is clearly not just an altered state of consciousness, since it can last from several months to many years. For its duration, the individual passes in and out of different states of consciousness— from wakefulness to sleeping and dreaming, and also to super- lucidity in any of these states. The entire process falls, in fact, outside the categories of "normal" and "psychotic." A person undergoing this striking psychophysiological transformation has experiences that are far from normal, though usually without becoming so disorganized as to be considered psychotic.

Neither is the kundalini process necessarily connected with the appearance of psychic phenomena. There are psychics who have not undergone this transformation, just as there are those in whom the kundalini is activated but who show no particular psychic talent. That is to say, the kundalini process may—and often does—lead to many special abilities, but it is not intrinsically tied to them. This is supported, for instance, by Swami Vishnu Tirtha (1962). He pointed out that a Yoga master who has control over his heart activity may still not have an awakened kundalini, whereas this and similar abilities may well be absent in an adept of Kundalini Yoga.

Finally, what does this transformative process mean? How are we to understand its curious patterns and phenomena? Clearly, the person undergoing this transformative process is likely to attach all kinds of significances to it. These can be expected to be highly personal and subjective. By contrast, my aim in this book is to describe the kundalini process in terms of what is observable.

In the present volume I present a series of cases, some of which are drawn from a survey of diverse cultures and spiritual traditions, while others derive from my own clinical experience as a psy- chiatrist. Both "samples" give us ample data for a rounded portrayal of psychophysiological transmutation.

Ordinarily a clinician may present his or her cases with the expectation that they will be accepted more or less at face value, even though the conclusions may be challenged. When I was preparing the first edition of this book, in 1976, the climate of medical opinion was such that I had many qualms about publishing my findings. Although the dominant scientific paradigm is still intolerant of the realities encountered in the kundalini process and spirituality in general, there have been many encouraging developments during the past decade or so. These support an enlarged view of the human being, which takes at least our psychic capacities, if not our spiritual destiny, into account. I wish to mention specifically the works by Kenneth Pelletier (1977), Larry Dossey (1982), and Gabriel Cousens (1986). I am, therefore, not in the least hesitant about reissuing my book in the present thoroughly revised and expanded form.

Of course, the model proposed here—which is essentially that formulated by Itzhak Bentov—is still subject to review and improvement. In the intervening years no more convincing model has come to my attention, but this does not mean that a new and better model could not be elaborated. The initial flurry of scientific interest in the kundalini process unfortunately did not lead to sustained and serious research into this important phenomenon. With the death of Itzhak Bentov in 1981 and Pandit Gopi Krishna in 1986, kundalini research has lost its most ardent advocates. It remains to be seen how this embryonic field of investigation will develop.

As for the present book, two interconnected theses are strongly argued. The first is that a process of psychophysiological transmutation, most usefully viewed as the "awakening of the kundalini," is indeed a reality. The second is that this process is part of an evolutionary mechanism and that as such it must not be viewed as a pathological development. Rather, I will strongly propose that the kundalini process is an aspect of human psychospiritual unfolding that is intrinsically desirable.

The evolutionary potential of the kundalini process has nowhere been vocalized more than in the writings of Gopi Krishna (1973). On the basis of firsthand experience of his own awakened kundalini, he made this statement:

> A new center—presently dormant in the average man and woman—has to be activated and a more powerful stream of psychic energy must rise into the head from the base of the spine to enable human consciousness to transcend the normal limits. This is the final phase of the present evolutionary impulse in man. The cerebrospinal system of man has to undergo a radical change, enabling consciousness to transcend the limits of the highest intellect. Here reason yields to intuition and Revelation appears to guide the steps of humankind. (p. 15)

I will begin my presentation by discussing the special significance of the transformative process today and by briefly reviewing the problem of objectivity in the description of psychospiritual states. Then I will look at the kundalini as it has been conceptualized in the Tantra Yoga tradition, since it is this traditional model that is best known and also more refined than other comparable models. It is, furthermore, quite amenable to a physiological interpretation. However, certain differences between the classical descriptions of the kundalini and my own data will lead me to distinguish between the traditional kundalini concept as "spiritual energy" and what I call the *physio*-kundalini.

In explaining the physio-kundalini, I will use, as already mentioned, Itzhak Bentov's model. It is the first (and so far only) model of the kundalini phenomenon subject to experimental verification. The significance of Bentov's work will be discussed, and his original paper on micromotion and the kundalini is included as Appendix 1. In my discussion of diagnosis, I will show that it is possible to recognize the physio-kundalini process and to distinguish it from psychosis, even when these two conditions are temporarily co-present in a particular individual. This distinction will help make it possible for clinicians to avoid the serious mistakes that have been made in the past. A faulty diagnosis can not only further complicate a case, but also deprive the person who has all the symptoms of an awakening or awakened kundalini of the great transformative and spiritual potential this signals.

Individuals undergoing the kundalini transformation often need special help, and I will consider which forms of help are advisable and which are not. Finally, I will suggest an approach for coping with the problems and opportunities generated by the kundalini phenomenon in society as a whole. Here, I feel, we can be guided by the precedent of Meher Baba's work with the Masts in India (see Appendix 2).

The concluding chapter was added to this new edition because I wanted to say something about the spiritual relevance of the kundalini phenomenon. I believe that there is a great deal of confusion about what authentic spirituality is in relation to the whole realm of psychic experiences. The teaching of the contemporary adept Da Love-Ananda (Da Free John) can serve us in our attempt to disentangle the many misconceptions of the popular mind and to put the kundalini phenomenon in its proper spiritual context.

Appendix 3 poses the fundamental question: Why is the transformative process possible at all? Appendices 4 and 5 are for the use of medical clinicians and specialists respectively.

Although the original version of this book was written with medical practitioners in mind, it was widely read by many non-specialists. Judging from the numerous letters and phone calls from my readers, the book has proved helpful to them. I hope that in its present revised and expanded form it will be even more useful to many more people.

ACKNOWLEDGMENTS

This book is, to a large extent, the product of a group effort. In particular, the author wishes to thank Keith Borden, Freda Morris, Henry S. Dakin, Gabriel Cousens, Danniel Kientz, Jean Millay, Richard Lowenberg, Elaine Chernoff, Beverly Johnson, George Meek, James Fadiman, and Itzhak Bentov for their advice and assistance in preparing, editing, and reviewing the manuscript and artwork for the first edition, and Shirley Triest and Matt Barna for their help with the cover on this new edition.

The participation of many other individuals in the research described in this volume is also gratefully acknowledged, though for reasons of privacy their names are not given.

Chapter 1

THE SIGNIFICANCE OF PSYCHOPHYSIOLOGICAL TRANSFORMATION TODAY

H alf a century ago, in a seminar on the kundalini, C. G. Jung (1932) and his colleagues observed that the awakening of this force had rarely, if ever, been witnessed in the West. They suggested, ironically, that it would take a thousand years for the kundalini to be set in motion by depth analysis. It is hard to believe that the kundalini phenomenon was unknown in premodern Europe, given the long-standing fascination with alchemy (as a psychospiritual discipline) and magic. Can we seriously believe that the ancient Druids, who were magi and hierophants, were ignorant of this force? Or that the mystics of ancient and medieval Christendom never experienced the phenomena accompanying its arousal? It is easier to concede that modern depth analysis might require a millennium for it to effect a kundalini awakening.

However remote Jung considered the possibility of an accidental or voluntary arousal of the kundalini in his day, he certainly had a clear grasp of its psychological significance. He told the allegory of a medieval monk who took a fantasy journey into a wild, unknown forest where he lost his way. While trying to retrace his steps, he found his path barred by a fierce dragon. Jung contended that this beast is the symbol of the kundalini, the force that, in psychological terms, obliges a person to go on his or her greatest adventure—the adventure of self-knowledge. One can only turn back at the cost of sacrificing the momentum of self-discovery and self-understanding, which would amount to a loss of meaning, purpose, and consciousness.

The awakening of the kundalini signals one's entry into the unknown forest of hidden dimensions of human existence. As Jung (1932) put it:

> When you succeed in awakening the kundalini, so that it starts to move out of its mere potentiality, you necessarily start a world which is totally different from our world. (p. 110)

Jung went on to describe the kundalini as an impersonal force, which is in consonance with the Hindu sources. He argued that to claim the kundalini experience as one's own creation is perilous. It leads to ego inflation, false superiority, obnoxiousness, or even madness. For him, the kundalini is an autonomous process arising out of the unconscious and seemingly using the individual as its vehicle.

This transmutative process was, admittedly, rare when Jung first considered it. This is no longer the case. Today kundalini awakenings occur more frequently, with and without training. What has happened? Some might argue that there has not really been any increase in kundalini cases at all, but that the intellectual climate has changed and people speak more freely about such experiences. There may be some truth in this, but I venture to suggest that there is another, more significant cause: People experience kundalini phenomena more frequently because they are actually more involved in disciplines and life-styles conducive to psychospiritual transformation.

Since the LSD revolution of the 1960s, the employment of nonrational (not merely irrational!) methods of awareness expansion or intensification has become increasingly acceptable, even fashionable, in certain sectors of our Western society. New therapies involving some form of meditative practice have sprung up. Hundreds of thousands of people, we are informed, practice Transcendental Meditation (TM). Many are engaged in Yoga, Vedanta, and the different schools of Buddhism—Zen, Vajrayana, Mahayana, Theravada. An even larger number of people pursue psychic arts, like dowsing, "channeling" (mediumism), magic, witchcraft, and psychic healing. And many more have a passive interest in, if not fascination for, such matters.

Some sociologists speak of an "occult revival" in our times, others of an "East-West encounter," while still others warn of the "new narcissism." Most commentators note that our Western civilization is in a state of profound ferment. A growing number of critics read our situation as one of crisis, whose outcome may well determine the destiny of humanity as a whole.

Jung (1964), for instance, pointed out that a period of dissociation is at once an age of death and rebirth. He referred to the end of the Roman Empire as paralleling our own era. Anticipating the revolutionary insights of Ilya Prigogine (1984), Jung remarked:

> . . . When one principle reaches the height of its power, the counter-principle is stirring within it like a germ. (p. 142)

What that principle is which is presently being replaced by its counter-principle, we can learn from the works of Lewis Mumford (1954), Pierre Teilhard de Chardin (1959), Theodore Roszak (1971), Charles A. Reich (1971), Morris Berman (1984), and Jean Gebser (1985). They are among those who champion the idea of an emerging "new age" or new consciousness. And that new consciousness supersedes what Gebser styles the "rational consciousness," with its rigid left-brain orientation to life and its anxious defense of the ego as the measure of all things.

The French psychiatrist Jacques Lacan has described the ego as a "paranoid construct" by which self and other are kept apart. This is precisely the orientation that underlies the whole scientific enterprise with its insistence on splitting value from fact, feeling from thinking—amounting to a "disenchantment" of the world, as Morris Berman (1984) has termed it. However, this entire orientation stands challenged by modern quantum theory and other avant-garde disciplines of science. More than anything, it has been called into question by the very life-style to which it has given rise and of which it is an integral part—our deeply troubled Western civilization.

The ego-bound rational consciousness is ultimately unfit for life. Not that there is anything intrinsically wrong with the ego or with reason. But where they are made the principles by which life is lived, they become destructive. The ego is a necessary stage in the development of the human personality, yet it is by no means its crowning accomplishment. Similarly, reason or rationality is an intrinsic quality or power of the human being. But it is only one among many capacities, and it is by no means the most important one. In fact, both ego and reason are recent appearances in the history of consciousness. And both are destined to be surpassed by superior forms of existence.

The search for meaning and happiness, which occupies a growing number of Westerners, is the other side of their profound dissatisfaction with the prevalent values, attitudes, and forms of life. It is, in the last analysis, a quest for that which lies beyond the boundaries of the ego and reason. Unfortunately, this journey often leads not to a transcendence of the ego and rationality, but to an immature denial of individuality that is accompanied, paradoxically, by narcissistic preoccupations, ego inflation, and an angry rejection of reason. This is evident in much of the contemporary preoccupation with spiritualism, witchcraft, and magic.

I have also witnessed this regrettable tendency among those who have stumbled onto the kundalini experience. But this says nothing about the experience itself, which is not inherently regressive. On the contrary, I view the kundalini awakening as an experience that fundamentally serves self-transcendence and mind-transcendence. I tend to agree with Gopi Krishna's (1971) appraisal of the kundalini. He wrote:

> This mechanism, known as Kundalini, is the real cause of all so-called spiritual and psychic phenomena, the biological basis of evolution and development of personality, the secret origin of all esoteric and occult doctrines, the master key to the unsolved mystery of creation, the inexhaustible source of philosophy, art and science, and the fountainhead of all religious faiths, past, present and future. (p. 124)

But while I regard the kundalini as the evolutionary engine par excellence, I do not wish to equate it with the ultimate reality of existence.

Chapter 2

THE KUNDALINI EXPERIENCE AND SCIENTIFIC OBJECTIVITY

Personal accounts of the awakening of the kundalini tend to be full of references to emotions, unusual thought processes, and visions, while physical signs and symptoms or *actual* sensations are rarely mentioned. Similarly, vague allusions to subjectively felt energy states and force fields make up most of the descriptions of meditative experiences.

For the most part, these accounts merely reiterate standard expectations and formulaic metaphors. Jung (1975) referred to the adherence to traditional models as a dogmatism that has its origin in the teacher-disciple relationship. Here the teacher communicates, both in words and often through direct initiation, the esoteric knowledge or vision that the disciple is to discover for himself or herself. In other words, the teacher provides a framework of interpretation that then serves the acolyte as a guiding light in his or her own psychospiritual journey.

Since intellectual analysis is typically downplayed in traditional schools of esotericism, the disciple tends to make the teacher's conceptual framework his or her own, without always looking at the fit between that framework and his or her actual experiencing. And even more independent-minded students, who question the inherited framework of explanation, are seldom willing to make radical innovations. It usually takes an accomplished adept and rounded personality of the stature of a Gautama the Buddha or a Jesus of Nazareth to break with tradition in a more obvious way.

The dependence on traditional explanations can clearly be seen in the classical accounts of the kundalini experience, as set forth in the Sanskrit scriptures of Yoga, notably Hatha Yoga. While this tendency is readily apparent in Eastern writings, it is also true of Western descriptions of psychospiritual processes. We have so far failed to clarify the different states of the psyche and the body in regard to "transcendental" or mystical experiences. There is as yet no commonly accepted phenomenology that would allow us to comprehend such states analytically and comprehensively.

For example, William James (1929) saw in the great German mystic Suso a suffering ascetic incapable of turning his torments into religious ecstasy. He wrote:

> His case is distinctly pathological, but he does not seem to have had the alleviation, which some ascetics have enjoyed, of an alteration of sensibility capable of actually turning torment into a perverse kind of pleasure. (p. 248)

By contrast, Jung (1932) and his colleagues thought Suso had experienced the kundalini process. These contrasting views would appear to reflect the different interests that James and Jung brought to their study of Suso. James was sensitive to the pathological element in religious and mystical life, whereas Jung was primarily concerned with the relationship between individuation and the kundalini.

Both James and Jung subscribed to the scientific ideal of objectivity. Nevertheless, both approached the subject of religious experience principally through comparative analysis rather than rigorous personal experimentation or laboratory testing of suitable volunteers. There is, of course, a place for both comparative analysis and experimentation. It is, however, chiefly by means of the latter— either in the form of self-experimentation or the experimental study of others—that we can hope to expose (and transcend) our own biases and preconceptions about psychospiritual processes.

In particular, such an "objective" approach can do away with the common presupposition that psychospiritual states have nothing to do with the body. This specific bias belongs to the age-old tradition of dualism, which conceives of a split between body and mind or body and spirit. Modern psychology and medicine have found the old scientific paradigm of Cartesianism to be inadequate. After denying for several decades the significance and even the reality of consciousness, these disciplines are now in the process of reconsidering the very premises on which they have been based. In a nutshell, they are coming to the conclusion that body and mind form a dynamic unity or are polar aspects of a larger reality.

This switch is best captured in the humanistic psychology of Abraham Maslow. In one of his landmark essays, he argued that the classical conception of objectivity works tolerably well only in regard to inanimate objects and, perhaps, lower organisms. When it comes to the animal kingdom and to human beings, the detachment of the cool observer is, as Maslow recognized, virtually impossible. While it is possible to eliminate some of our preconceptions through intense self-examination, Maslow (1983) held that the best possible avenue was to marshal our capacity for love in order to know and understand other beings "objectively." He wrote:

> To the extent that it is possible for us to be non-intrusive, non-demanding, non-hoping, non-improving, to that extent do we achieve this particular kind of objectivity. (p. 18)

In the 1950s scientists began to study "altered states" of consciousness in the laboratory. The first experiments involved the electroencephalographic (EEG) study of yogins and Zen practitioners. Later, in the 1960s and 1970s, many similar studies were made of TM practitioners. Other tests were also devised to track down the physiological correlates of these elusive psychospiritual processes. They included measurements of heart activity and skin resistance.

Researchers also encouraged more open and immediate accounts of personal experiencing, focusing in particular on somatic changes. This procedure has led to the important discovery that there is a whole range of phenomena in the process of psychospiritual transformation that are constant and universal, transcending personal and cultural differences. This is no less than traditionalists have claimed. It is now possible, however, to begin to distinguish more carefully between personal idiosyncracies and predictable patterns. This is especially important in view of the fact that today the kundalini experience does not occur exclusively in an esoteric setting where the teacher monitors the pupil's progress.

The uniform aspects of the kundalini experience, furthermore, are a potent indication that the experience is not illusory but real.

The signs and symptoms usually described, such as shifts in emoting and thinking as well as the experience of visions and the hearing of voices, appear to be largely determined by personal factors (the "set") and external circumstances (the "setting"). But such physical sensations as itching, fluttering, tingling, intense heat and cold, photisms (perceptions of inner lights) and the perception of primary sounds, as well as the occurrence of spasms and contortions, seem to be "archetypal" features of the process, or at least of certain phases of it. It is this universality that leads me to postulate that all psychospiritual practices activate the same basic process, and that this process has a definite physiological basis.

Yet, clearly, the emotional aspect of psychophysiological transformation must not be underrated, for it is the source of the personal meanings that each individual experiences in relation to the transformative process. Together with the alterations in the thinking process, the emotional changes have frequently been mistaken for mental illness. But, as I have already explained, to interpret the kundalini experience as a psychotic state is unwarranted. Although the experience may include pathological episodes or aspects, these must be understood in the context of the totality of the individual's life and the meaningfulness of the kundalini experience itself.

The subjective dimension of the psychospiritual process is richly varied, ranging over a broad spectrum of experiential phenomena—from helpless confusion and depression to self-transcending ecstasy and blissful superlucidity. The compelling quality of these emotional states tends to overshadow the physiological details, so that the experiencer of the kundalini process is apt to ignore the subtle changes occurring in his or her physical condition. But whereas the intellectual-emotional component of the transmutative process is highly diversified, the somatic component is more amenable to systematic study. For the reasons already stated, I will focus on the physiological parameters of the kundalini arousal, reading them in terms of the model developed by Itzhak Bentov.

Chapter 3

THE KUNDALINI EXPERIENCE—
THE CLASSICAL MODEL

E very spiritual tradition has its own model of the transformative
process. Generally these models stress the subjective side of the
experience, treating the objective signs as incidental or ignoring
them altogether. Thus the traditional descriptions of psychospiritual
metamorphosis, valid as they may be to initiates, are none too
helpful in making objective comparisons and in arriving at an overall
appraisal of the process. In physiological terms, most of these
models have little relevance.

There are, however, important exceptions, notably the Tantra
Yoga model of the kundalini experience. According to this Indian
tradition, the kundalini is a type of energy—a "power" or "force"
(*shakti*)—that is held to rest in a dormant, or potential, state in the
human body. Its location is generally specified as being at the base of
the spine. When this energy is galvanized, "awakened," it rushes
upward along the central axis of the human body, or along the spinal
column, to the crown of the head. Occasionally it is thought to go
even beyond the head. Upon arriving there, the kundalini is said to
give rise to the mystical state of consciousness, which is inde-
scribably blissful and in which all awareness of duality ceases.

According to Tantra Yoga metaphysics, the kundalini resident
in the individual human body is an aspect of the transcendental
Power that precedes and yet also pervades the entire cosmos. It *is*
that Power. But this realization is only made when the kundalini has
fully ascended from the bodily base to its optimal position at the

crown of the head, or beyond. Tantra Yoga understands this whole process as a play between the two fundamental aspects of the ultimate Reality. One aspect is called the "Power," or Shakti, and the other is God Shiva. The Sanskrit word *shiva* means literally "tranquil." In Tantra Yoga it refers to the static (masculine) pole or aspect of the ultimate Reality, whereas the word *shakti* designates the dynamic (feminine) pole. Shiva stands for pure, object-transcending and self-transcending Consciousness, and Shakti stands for the world-creating Power of Consciousness.

On the transcendental level, both aspects are forever inseparable. Shiva and Shakti are always in ecstatic embrace. But on the level of normal human consciousness, they appear separated. Hence the ordinary individual has only a trickle of that transcendental Power available, just as he or she experiences only a fraction of that transcendental Consciousness, in the form of individuated awareness.

Sir John Woodroffe (1929), alias Arthur Avalon, who pioneered the study of Tantra Yoga, offered this explanation:

> Whatever is felt and known, hoped and wished, in fact all the varied experiences of the limited self, appear and disappear, rise and fall, like waves in an infinite sea of Consciousness . . . Man's spiritual existence is never at any moment simply the aggregate of the modes of experience that he may have at that moment. For pragmatic reasons, he commonly ignores many of the modes themselves: he is commonly partial to a few and regards these as all that he possesses at that moment. But these are not all that is ignored; what is generally ignored, though it cannot be ever for a single moment effaced or shut out, is the placid background or atmosphere of Consciousness in which all appearances take place . . . This indeed is the quiescent, placid aspect of man's being—the *Shiva* aspect. Against it we have the stressing, dynamical, moving and changing aspect—the *Shakti* aspect . . . (pp. 41–42)

He explained further:

> Power is that aspect of Consciousness in which it stresses and changes as the world-order. As such changing action is commonly called action or movement, Power is regarded as the moving, acting, dynamical aspect of Consciousness. If Consciousness which is is the essence of Power, be veiled, that is

unrecognised, then Power is the creative Impulse that continuously changes as the world—there being no rest, no endurance,
no permanence . . . But it is essentially a Power of Consciousness
. . . Not only does *Shakti* presuppose *Shiva; Shakti* is *Shiva.*
(p. 50)

Elsewhere Woodroffe (1978) observed that the "doctrine of
Shakti is a profound one," which is "likely to be attractive to
Western minds when they have grasped it" (p. 119). He was not
mistaken, for lately we encounter the Shiva-Shakti metaphor in the
literature of the "new physics." It took the revolutionary findings of
quantum physics for Western scientists to begin to appreciate
Eastern cosmological thinking, which views reality as a process of
polar dynamics that unfolds against the backdrop of a single
continuum. This reality appears to be not material but supermaterial
or, as some avant-garde physicists argue, supermaterial and
superconscious.

Like all ancient teachings, Tantra Yoga looks upon the individual human being as a faithful reflection of the macrocosm. The
universal, nonlocal Power is present in the human body-mind at a
"location" corresponding to the anal region. This is the position of
the first of seven principal centers or seats of Power arrayed along
the body's axis. These centers or *cakras* ("wheels")—often spelled
"chakras"—are commonly depicted as lotus flowers with varying
numbers of petals said to correspond to different forms of energy
associated with each center. These foci are, as it were, the organs or
limbs of the Power. They are localized vortices of bioenergy.

The center at the anus bears the technical name of "root-prop
center" *(muladhara-cakra).* It is traditionally held to be associated
with the earth element, the sense of smell, the feet, and the general
distribution of the life-force *(prana)* in the body.

The second center in ascending order is the so-called
svadhishthana-cakra, which is located in the genital area. The name
is, like many esoteric Sanskrit terms, difficult to translate. It means
roughly "own-standing center," referring to the genitals as the most
obvious characteristic of the human body. This focal point of the
Power is thought to be associated with the traditional water element,
the sense of taste, the hands, and sexuality.

The third center is called *manipura-cakra* or "center of the gem city." It is situated in the region of the navel, which, in some traditions, is given as an alternative resting-place for the dormant kundalini. This center is commonly said to be connected with the traditional fire element, digestion, the anus, and, curiously, with the sense of sight.

The fourth center, at the heart, is frequently referred to as the "heart lotus" *(hrit-padma)* but also as the *anahata-cakra*. The word *anahata* means literally "unstruck" and is an esoteric designation for the eternal sound *om*. This sound is not generated by any causal mechanisms, but the experienced yogin can perceive it by focusing his attention on the heart lotus. This center is explained as being associated with the traditional air element, the sense of touch, feelings, the genitals, and the stimulation of the life-force.

The fifth center, which is situated at the throat, is known as the *vishuddhi-cakra* or "center of purity." It is said to be connected with the traditional ether element, the sense of hearing, the mouth, and the skin.

The sixth center, depicted as a two-petaled lotus located at the forehead between the brows, is the *ajna-cakra* or "command center." It is also known as the "third eye." It is commonly regarded as being associated with the mind *(manas)*. It is in this center that the teacher is said to contact the disciple telepathically.

The seventh and final center of this main sequence is the *sahasrara-cakra*. The word *sahasrara* is composed of *sahasra*, meaning "thousand," and *ara*, meaning "spoke." The thousand spokes or energy pathways of this center, which is located at the crown of the head, are representative of the experience of overwhelming light and bliss that results when the kundalini force rises from the lowest center to the crown center. In the Sanskrit literature, this center is described as "lustrous," "whiter than the full moon," "shedding a constant and profuse stream of nectar." Gopi Krishna (1971) confirmed this:

> Whenever I turned my mental eye upon myself I invariably perceived a luminous glow within and outside my head in a state of constant vibration, as if a jet of an extremely subtle and brilliant substance rising through the spine spread itself out in

the cranium, filling and surrounding it with an indescribable radiance. (p. 87)

Light, as we shall see, is an important aspect of the kundalini awakening. It is one of the constants of psychospiritual experience and has been reported by mystics of all religious traditions.

Another important part of the Tantra Yoga model of the kundalini process is the notion of three major "ducts" or pathways along which the aroused kundalini force can travel. These are the so-called *nadis*. One is said to be experienced as a straight pathway connecting all the seven major centers. The other two wrap around it in helix fashion. The central "duct" is known as the *sushumna-nadi*. The channel starting to the left of it in the lowest center is called the *ida-nadi*, and the one starting to the right of it is called the *pingala-nadi*. The two helical channels pass each other at the various centers until they merge in the *ajna-cakra*.

According to traditional explanations, the right channel has a "heating" function, whereas the left channel is thought to "cool" the body. They clearly correspond, on the physiological plane, to the two nervous systems—the sympathetic and the parasympathetic respectively. I use the word "correspond" advisedly, because some Yoga authorities insist that the pathways cannot simply be identified with the nervous system. Rather they are subtle, esoteric phenomena to be experienced and understood only in a meditative state.

The scriptures of Tantrism and Hatha Yoga are very emphatic about the fact that, in order to avoid unpleasant and even dangerous side effects, the awakened kundalini must be guided through the central channel alone. As it ascends in it, the different centers become active and, according to some authorities, they actually come into existence only at that moment. As the aroused kundalini current passes through each center, it temporarily energizes it and then, as it moves on, absorbs its energy. By the time the kundalini force reaches the topmost center, the rest of the body is depleted of bioenergy. The lower extremities tend to become cold and corpselike.

This physiological phenomenon contrasts most strikingly with the intense experience of bliss, light, and superlucidity associated with the entry of the kundalini current into the topmost center. This experience is not one of catalepsy but of formless ecstasy or *nirvikalpa-samadhi*.

At first the full ascent of the kundalini force lasts for only a brief period, perhaps seconds or minutes. Then the kundalini moves back into one or the other lower center. It is the objective of Tantra Yoga to repeat this elevated state as often as possible, until the kundalini resides permanently in the crown center. The yogin is typically advised to consciously guide the descending kundalini and to have it come to rest not lower than the heart center. Kundalini activity in the lower three centers is commonly thought to be fraught with dangers, including ego inflation and rampant sexual desire.

The idea behind the arousal of the kundalini is that it includes the body in the process of psychospiritual transformation. This is held to make the final ecstatic accomplishment more complete. In Tantra Yoga the body is not regarded as an obstacle to spiritual aspiration. It is looked upon as a temple of the Divine. One is reminded of Albert Einstein's (1949) remark that "those who would preserve the spirit must also look after the body to which it is attached" (p. 102). This meshes with the great Tantric doctrine that the unconditional Reality *(nirvana)* and finite existence *(samsara)* are ultimately identical. This identity is discovered when limited self-consciousness is transcended in yogic ecstasy.

Chapter 4

THE PHYSIO-KUNDALINI

The arousal of the kundalini power is a dramatic occurrence. It is traditionally looked upon as a mighty process of purification that leads to the transcendence of the body and the mind in the culminating state of ecstatic unification of subject and object.

In the course of its upward motion, the kundalini is held to encounter all kinds of impurities that are burned off by its dynamic activity. In particular, the Sanskrit scriptures mention three major structural blockages, known as "knots." According to traditional understanding, these knots are located at the lowest center in the anal area, the heart center, and the center between and behind the eyebrows. The yogin is instructed to pierce through each knot by way of single-minded concentration and focused breath.

But the pathway of the kundalini can be blocked anywhere along its upward trajectory. We can look upon these blockages as stress points. Thus, in its ascent, the kundalini causes the central nervous system to throw off stress. This is usually associated with the experience of pain. When the kundalini encounters these blocks, it works away at them until they are dissolved. This best demonstrates the self-directing behavior of the aroused kundalini. It appears to act of its own volition, spreading through the entire psychophysiological system to effect its transformation.

Once a blockage is removed, the kundalini flows freely through that point and continues its upward journey until it meets with the next area of stress. Moreover, the kundalini energy appears to diffuse, so that it may be operating on several levels at once, removing several different stress points simultaneously.

31

The kundalini moves inexorably upward until it reaches the center at the crown of the head. However diffuse the kundalini energy may have been in the course of its ascent, once the topmost center is reached it becomes focused. We can understand this process as being analogous to the phenomenon of electricity. An electrical current produces light when it passes through a thin tungsten filament, but not when it travels through a thick copper wire, because the filament offers appreciable resistance while the wire does not. Similarly, the kundalini produces the most striking sensations when it encounters a part of the psychophysiological system that offers particular resistance. But the "heat" generated by the "friction" of the kundalini against this resistance soon "burns out" the blockage, and then the sensations cease.

There is another way of looking at this process: An intense flow of water through a small rubber hose will cause the hose to whip about violently, whereas the same flow through a fire hose will scarcely be noticeable. Likewise, the flow of the kundalini energy through restricted areas of the body-mind causes turbulence, which may be experienced as painful sensations. Of course, these are all only metaphors. The actual kundalini process is undoubtedly far more subtle and complex than either electricity or water rushing through a hose.

However, it is possible to understand a whole range of kundalini phenomena in strictly physiological and physical terms. This is exactly what Itzhak Bentov, whose model accounts for much of what I and others have observed about the kundalini process, has done. The spontaneous bodily movements, shifting somatic sensations, and other phenomena reported in the following cross-cultural survey and case studies can all readily be interpreted as by-products of kundalini activity. And Bentov's model offers the best explanation available.

I need to emphasize, however, that there are differences between my clinical observations and the classical model of the kundalini process. The most striking difference concerns the movement of the kundalini energy through the body-mind. According to the traditional scriptures of Yoga and Tantrism, the kundalini rises from the center at the base of the spine along the spinal axis to the crown of the head. This description is also part of the self-reports of Swami Muktananda (1974) and Gopi Krishna (1971). By contrast, my clinical data and also some traditional non-Hindu accounts point to a movement of the kundalini proceeding from the feet and legs along the back of the trunk or along the spine to the head and from there down over the face, through the throat, and terminating in the abdomen.

Thus in Taoist Yoga, as described by Charles Luk (1972), alias Lu K'uan Yü, the "microcosmic orbit" of the inner fire begins at the base of the spine, rises to the brain, and from there returns to its starting point. This is entirely in accord with predictions from Bentov's model.

The question now is: How is the difference between Bentov's model and the classical kundalini model to be explained? Two main possibilities suggest themselves. One may assume that two related but essentially different processes are at work here. Or one may assume that the underlying process is the same and that the differences are merely incidental. The first assumption is less likely, since the descriptions are too similar. If the second explanation is correct, which I suggest, one still needs to account for the differences.

One can speculate that the differences could simply be due to incorrect or inadequate self-observation and description. Could it be that those who have had spontaneous kundalini awakenings without knowledge of the classical Hindu explanations simply did not have the right language to express what they were experiencing? Or could it be that those pursuing kundalini arousal in the context of the classical model somehow overdetermine their experiences? The second explanation seems to me to be far more likely. Language structures our experience. Once we have accepted a particular model as a faithful reflection of reality, we cease to think of it in terms of a model and instead equate it with reality.

The yogin who applies himself to the age-old techniques of kundalini arousal inevitably does so on the basis of the classical model of the kundalini. He fully expects the kundalini energy to awaken in the basal center and to travel upward to the crown center, where it generates untold bliss. It is therefore very likely that he would ignore any phenomena that do not fit the prescription. More than that, he may not even consciously experience any such phenomena, because his attention is focused on a different aspect of the total process.

By the same token, it seems highly likely that those who undergo spontaneous kundalini awakenings, without preconceived notions about this process, are the better observers. They would notice phenomena that, from the classical viewpoint, have no significance or do not even exist. They do not hold in their heads the yogin's elaborate metaphysical framework, which acts as a reality filter. Hence they are more sensitive to the unique manifestations of the kundalini experience, certainly on the somatic level.

At the same time, however, they are apt to be at a disadvantage when it comes to exploring the deeper spiritual possibilities of the process. The reason is that, lacking the classical background, they are also unfamiliar with the full kundalini potential as it has been realized by some adepts. Indeed, they may subscribe to the materialistic philosophy that forms the backbone of our Western civilization, and in this case they would not even consider their experience in a higher light. Instead, they would fear—as many of my clients have done—for their own sanity.

The kundalini process holds many secrets. There is much that I as a physician do not understand about it. Therefore it seems advisable to focus on those aspects about which something useful can be said. And this is the physiological dimension of the kundalini experience. I propose to apply the term *physio-kundalini* to those aspects of the kundalini process which can be accounted for in purely physiological terms. The physio-kundalini is, then, the slow progression of energy sensation originating in the lower part of the body and rising through it into the head and proceeding down through the throat into the abdomen where this stimulus reaches its culmination point. I will also refer to this complex phenomenon as the *physio-kundalini process* or *cycle* or *mechanism*.

When the kundalini energy encounters a resistance in its path and then overcomes it and purifies the psychophysiological system of that block, I will speak of an *opening* of that particular location. The opening of the throat is a typical example. This terminology is adequately descriptive and amenable to physiological interpretation. It even offers contact points with the classical model of the kundalini process, without committing us to metaphysical and idealized descriptions of that model.

Chapter 5

CROSS-CULTURAL ASPECTS OF THE KUNDALINI EXPERIENCE

The !Kung of Africa

Northwest Botswana is the home of the !Kung people of the Kalahari Desert. The American anthropologist Richard Katz (1973) has given us an insightful account of the mystical practices of these people. He described how the !Kung dance for many hours in order to "heat up" the n/um so that the !kia state can be attained. Katz noted that n/um is analogous to the kundalini. !Kia is the condition of transcendence. This state goes beyond what is generally called a "peak experience," in which the ordinary waking consciousness is temporarily transcended to make room for ecstatic feelings ("highs"). It is more what Abraham Maslow (1973) termed "plateau experience," in which one's whole being participates, consciously (or supraconsciously) and joyously, in the larger life, and which is thoroughly transformative. The !kia condition is thus similar to the Zen *satori* or certain forms of Indian *samadhi* that are not necessarily accompanied by a loss of sensory awareness.

The !Kung tribesman who has been initiated into the secrets of n/um is taught how to arouse this power and how to conquer the inevitable fear he will encounter in the face of the tremendous inner force that threatens to eclipse his self-sense. Once he has crossed over this threshold of fear, he enters the !kia state.

N/um is said to reside in the pit of the stomach. As it warms up, it rises from the base of the spine to the skull, and it is there that the !kia state is attained. According to Katz (1973), one tribesman offered this report:

> You dance, dance, dance, dance. Then n/um lifts you in your belly and lifts you in your back, and then you start to shiver. N/um makes you tremble; it's hot. Your eyes are open but you don't look around; you hold your eyes still and look straight ahead. But when you get into !kia, you're looking around because you see everything, because you see what's troubling everybody . . . Rapid shallow breathing, that's what draws n/um up . . . then n/um enters every part of your body, right to the tip of your feet and even your hair. (p. 140)

Another tribesman put it this way:

> In your backbone you feel a pointed something, and it works its way up. Then the base of your spine is tingling, tingling, tingling, tingling, tingling, tingling, tingling . . . and then it makes your thoughts nothing in your head. (p. 140)

At the height of the !kia state, a n/um master can perform a variety of extraordinary feats, such as curing the sick and handling or walking on fire. He may also develop remote vision, enabling him to see over vast distances. One n/um master said that when he is in the !kia state, "I can really become myself again," implying that these different paranormal abilities are natural human capacities.

By transcending his ordinary consciousness and self-sense, a n/um master is, above all, able to contact the supernatural realm and combat the ghosts that, in !Kung cosmology, are responsible for illness. The struggle with these ghosts is at the heart of the n/um master's art, skill, and power. Healing is, for him, a matter of winning the battle against the personified forces that cause sickness.

As Katz pointed out, the !Kung seek !kia not merely for their own personal enrichment, but primarily to help others. Nor is the !kia state sought as a permanent refuge from ordinary life. On the contrary, a tribesman is expected to soon return to the ordinary state and its responsibilities. An extended !kia is not seen as a state of grace but as a mistake. !Kia is to be sought for entering the sacred dimension of existence, receiving its nourishment, and then sharing with one's fellow beings what has been received in the process of healing.

The sole criterion for determining who becomes an adept in the n/um process is the process itself. Every individual who experiences n/um and is able to attain the !kia condition is automatically considered to be a n/um master. It is recognized that the more feeling a person is and the richer his powers of imagination are, the more likely he is to !kia, that is, to transcend his ordinary state. Over half the members of the !Kung tribe can attain the !kia state, and this ability seems to run in families.

The arousal of n/um is connected with fear and pain, and it is quite unpredictable. The !Kung believe that a n/um master can create n/um in a student and also control the process so that the excessive fear that accompanies the arousal does not prevent the occurrence of !kia. The !Kung regard n/um as a gift from the gods, though it now passes from person to person.

Saint Thérèse, a Christian Mystic

In her autobiography, St. Thérèse of Lisieux (1962), who lived from 1873 to 1897, describes how she suffered phenomena that are similar to those observed in cases of spontaneous kundalini awakening. Thérèse hailed from a middle-class French family with apparently happily married parents and four sisters. At age ten she became a student at a nearby Carmelite convent. A few months after her enrollment she developed constant headaches. One evening, while preparing for bed, she began to shiver uncontrollably. These spells continued for a week and were uninfluenced by any treatment. The shivering was not accompanied by fever, and it disappeared as mysteriously as it had come.

A few weeks later, however, she was stricken with a "strange melange of hallucinations, comas, and convulsions." She appeared to be in delirium, crying out against unseen and terrifying creatures. She tossed violently in bed, hitting her head on the bedboards as if some strange force were assailing her. These "convulsions," which sometimes resembled the contortions of a gymnast, were occasionally so violent that she would be thrown out of bed. There were rotary or tumbling movements of her whole body that were quite beyond her normal flexibility. For instance, she would spring from her knees and stand on her head without the use of her hands. Later, during Mass, she had a more severe attack that ceased only after her earnest prayer.

What is, perhaps, most remarkable is the fact that despite these violent attacks, involving bizarre contortions and gyrations of the body, she was never physically harmed. On occasion she would plunge head first onto the floor or be dashed against the headboard of her bed and yet remain unhurt.

This strange illness lasted less than two months. Subsequently, two more incidents of fainting and rigidity occurred that lasted for only a few moments. Throughout all this, Thérèse claimed she never lost awareness, even during the "fainting" spell, but that she had no control over her bodily activity. In her own words:

> I was delirious nearly all the time and talking utter nonsense, and yet I'm quite certain that I never, for a moment, lost the use of my reason. Often I seemed to be in a dead faint, without making the slightest movement: anybody could do anything they liked with me—you could have killed me unresisting; and yet all the time I heard everything that was being said round me, and I remember it all still. (p. 89)

Saint Thérèse was attended regularly by a competent physician, who was unable to help her and frankly admitted to being confused by her symptoms. He was, however, firm in his opinion that it was not hysteria. Thérèse herself condemned her terrifying experiences as "the work of the devil." In retrospect, we may more benignly see in it the symptoms of a spontaneous kundalini arousal that were not properly understood. How many other saints in the Christian tradition underwent similar experiences for which neither medicine nor theology had any satisfactory explanation?

Psychosomatic Heat

Heat, as psychosomatic heat, makes its appearance in numerous religious traditions of the world. As Mircea Eliade (1968) observed:

Here we touch upon an extremely important problem concerning not only Indian religion but the history of religion in general: the excess of *power*, the magico-religious *force*, is experienced as a very vivid warmth. This is no longer a question of the *myths* and *symbols* of power, but of an experience which modifies the very physiology of the ascetic. There is every reason to believe that this experience was known by the mystics and magicians of the most ancient times. A great many "primitive" tribes conceive the magico-religious power as "burning" and express it by terms that signify "heat," "burn," "very hot" etc. (p. 147)

Eliade (1968) further noted:

It must be remembered, too, that all over the world shamans and sorcerers are reputedly "masters of fire," and swallow burning embers, handle red-hot iron and walk over fire. On the other hand they exhibit great resistance to cold. The shamans of the Arctic regions, as well as the ascetics of the Himalayas, thanks to their "magical heat," perform feats of resistance to cold that passes imagination. (p. 148)

Many traditions, notably Tibetan (Vajrayana) Buddhism and Chinese Taoism, have developed elaborate theories and practices revolving around the manipulation of the psychosomatic heat. In Tibet, for instance, the "Yoga of Heat *(tum-mo)*" is counted as one of the six great approaches to enlightenment. It is also valued by the Tibetan monks for its useful side effect of keeping them warm in the middle of winter. Masters of this Yoga are known to be able to dry wet sheets on their body at excessively low temperatures.

The Taoist tradition has developed a complex physiological alchemy which uses the inner heat *(huo)* to increase one's vitality, so as to accomplish the creation of the indestructible "diamond body."

Evelyn Underhill (1961), in her widely acclaimed study, mentions the "heat" experience of Richard Rolle of Hampole, "the father of English mysticism" (p. 193). In his work *Fire of Love* (I.14), Rolle wrote: "Heat soothly I call when the mind truly is kindled in Love Everlasting, and the heart on the same manner to burn not hopingly but verily is felt. The heart truly turned into fire, gives feeling of burning love." Rolle himself was amazed at the intensity of this experience, which was not purely mental or imaginary, but had a strong physical manifestation. In the prologue to his work he remarked that "oft have I groped my breast, seeing whether this burning were of any bodily cause outwardly."

The same painful sensation of heat is reported by a modern mystic, Irina Tweedie (1979), who was apprenticed by an Indian Sufi teacher. In her spiritual autobiography she has the following diary entry:

> Burning currents of fire inside; cold shivers running outside, along the spine, wave after wave, over legs, arms, abdomen, making all the hair rise. It is as if the whole frame were full of electricity. (p. 62)

Another entry reads:

> The power inside my body did not abate all night and I could not sleep. I noticed something completely new. My blood was getting luminous and I saw its circulation throughout the body. I soon then became aware that it was not the blood; a light, a bluish-white light was running along another system . . . The light came out of the body and re-entered it again at different points. Observing closely I could see that there were countless points of light like a luminous web encircling the body inside and out. It was very beautiful. No bones existed; the body was built on the web of light.
>
> Soon however I became aware that the body seemed to be on fire. This liquid light was cold but it was burning me, as if currents of hot lava were flowing through every nerve and every fibre, more and more unbearable and luminous, faster and faster. Shimmering, fluctuating, expanding and contracting, I could do nothing but lie there watching helplessly as the suffering and intense heat increased with every second . . . Burned alive. (p. 68)

Baneky Behari (1971) cites two examples from the Sufi literature that are also worth noting here because they involve a degree of externalization of that inner heat.

> Then the saint came to take a meal, and the girl was pouring water on his hands. She noticed that so intense was the fire of separation burning in him that immediately the water would fall on his hands it would pass into vapor. (p. 175)

By troth I see, as the physician tries to touch my hand, his hand is burnt and patches and swellings immediately appear on it. Such is the heat of the fire of separation. He alone knoweth my condition who hath endured such pain cheerfully when it fell to his lot. (p. 182)

Tony Agpaoa, a Philippine "psychic surgeon" who has received much public attention, told me in a conversation in 1974 that he had learned to ignite fires by mental means as part of his training as a healer. Swami Muktananda remarked in a personal communication in 1975 that this ability is part of the training in certain yogic schools. The widespread tradition of objective heat manifestation, I suggest, adds credence to similar manifestations in the clinical cases of kundalini awakening.

In recent times, many occurrences of "spontaneous combustion" have been reported. Hernani G. Andrade (1975), of the Brazilian Institute for Psychobiophysical Research, investigated many fires that occurred spontaneously. Some of them were witnessed by police officers. I myself experienced such a case.

I spent two years investigating poltergeist cases involving frequent fires (see Morris 1974). In one instance, the poltergeist phenomena occurred when a son was born to a young Jewish man and his Catholic wife. The intermarriage was surrounded by familial conflict, and the situation was highly charged emotionally. The poltergeist activity first centered on the baby, symbols of the marriage, and religious artifacts. Then the young husband decided to convert to Catholicism. This, together with the more and more disruptive poltergeist phenomena, threw the families into great turmoil.

The family members of four generations and several other people witnessed a range of paranormal events, including the spontaneous movement and disappearance of objects. The young couple suffered sensations of being struck, shaken, scratched, and choked. The girl's mother was struck and knocked unconscious one evening and had to be hospitalized.

There were a number of spontaneous fires witnessed by each family member and by several investigators. My first experience happened one evening when the grandfather went into the bedroom to check on the baby and found the curtains ablaze. He and I burned our hands slightly in putting the fire out. I was also present when several other small fires broke out. After the young man converted to Catholicism, avidly invested his energy in the Church, and secured an official exorcism, the phenomena ceased.

One may look upon these cases as possible examples of how pent-up psychosomatic energy can become externalized, since heat is one of the regular manifestations of an active kundalini. It is also more easily observed and measured than other physiological changes during this process. Upon reaching the crown center, the heat produced by the ascent of the kundalini makes way for the experience of intense luminosity as an accompaniment of ecstatic illumination.

The Experience of Light

The experience of light can be called a universal constant of spiritual or mystical experiencing. It is also associated with the ascent of the kundalini power into the crown center, or *sahasrara-cakra*. This is how Gopi Krishna (1971) described that phenomenon:

> Whenever I turned my mental eye upon myself I invariably perceived a luminous glow within and outside my head in a state of constant vibration, as if a jet of an extremely subtle and brilliant substance rising through the spine spread itself out in the cranium, filling and surrounding it with an indescribable radiance. (p. 87)

Swami Muktananda (1974) described a similar phenomenon:

> I looked all around. The flames of a vast conflagration were raging in all directions. The entire cosmos was on fire . . . I saw a dazzling brightness in my head and was terrified. (p. 63)

It is no accident that the highest mystical realization is generally referred to as "illumination" or "enlightenment." Mystics and realizers of all ages have spoken of the "radiance" aspect of their spiritual state, which is a literal experience for them.

The experience of the "inner light" is also an integral part of

Shamanism. Thus the Eskimos know of a mystical condition that they call *quaumaneq*, meaning "lightning" or "illumination," without which a man cannot become a shaman. This strange light fills the shaman's head and body, and it is thought to enable him to see at great distances, in the dark, and even into the future.

In the ancient *Chandogya-Upanishad*, one of the earliest esoteric scriptures of Hinduism, the transcendental Self is said to reside as the "inner light" in the region of the heart. According to Mahayana Buddhism, Gautama, the founder of Buddhism, awakened to the enlightened condition as he, after another night of watchful meditation, raised his eyes to the sky where he perceived the morning star. The star symbolizes the "Clear Light," or the universal reality beyond all forms. It is this Clear Light that the Tibetan Buddhist masters admonish the faithful to keep in their attention during the death process.

According to the *Lalita-Vistara*, a traditional biography of the Buddha, a ray of light would rise from the crown of Gautama's head whenever he sat absorbed in deepest meditation. This reminds one of a verse in the fourteenth chapter of the *Bhagavad-Gita*, which states that when there is real knowledge, or wisdom, the body emanates light. The same claim is made by the Chinese sage Chuang Tzu.

In the famous eleventh chapter of the *Bhagavad-Gita* there is a beautiful description of Prince Arjuna's enlightenment experience. He was overwhelmed by a vision of the radiant glory of God Krishna, symbolizing the ultimate reality. Arjuna experienced the Divine as a "mass of brilliance, flaming all round . . . entirely a brilliant radiance of sun-fire" (Feuerstein 1980, p. 118).

Not all experiences of nonphysical light necessarily indicate the ultimate condition of enlightenment, or perfect self-transcendence. The mystical traditions of the world also recognize so-called photistic experiences—or experiences of inner (and seemingly external) lights—without going beyond the subject-object division. The adepts of Hatha Yoga and Tantrism have developed complex visualization techniques in which photisms play an important role. They are taken as steps toward the realization of the uncreated Light.

Similarly the Taoist masters have elaborated practices for

"circulating" the inner light, by which the "Golden Flower" is opened and the "Elixir of Immortality" is obtained.

In early Christianity the rite of baptism was known as *photismos* or "illumination." The Holy Ghost came to be represented as a flame. As Christian legend has it, when Jesus was baptized in the river Jordan, the water was set on fire. According to an ancient tradition, a true monk literally shines with the "light of grace." Many stories are told of monks who, absorbed in prayer, would radiate light.

The Taoist Tradition

The kundalini phenomenon is well known in the Chinese Taoist tradition (see Lu K'uan Yü 1970). It is thought that after one has learned to achieve stillness of mind, hitherto dormant virtues or abilities will manifest themselves. The vital principle, known as *chi* (which is equivalent to the Sanskrit concept of *prana*), is accumulated in the lower belly through a variety of mental and bodily disciplines. When control over the mind is achieved, this chi or life-force bursts out and begins to flow in the main "channels" of the body, causing involuntary movements (physical automatisms). The conductivity of the chi is also said to produce the following eight sensations: pain, itching, coldness, warmth, weightlessness, heaviness, roughness, and smoothness.

The life-force is hot, and it not only spreads its heat to different parts of the body, but it may even become bright and perceptible to the meditator. In exceptional meditators it can occasionally cast an objectively visible light. When the life-force moves into obstructed areas, it induces painful and rather unpleasant sensations of roughness and cramping.

Lu K'uan Yü, alias Charles Luk, reported of the Taoist master Yin Shih Tsu as writing in 1914 that he felt heat going from the base of his spine to the top of his head, then down over his face and throat to his stomach. His whole body turned and twisted, and he saw a variety of internal lights (photisms). He had headaches, and one time his head felt swollen. The upper part of his body seemed to stretch so that he felt ten feet tall. This is spoken of as the "great body" in Buddhist scriptures.

Yin Shi Tsu remarked that he did not experience these various sensations all at once, but encountered one or the other of them at different times during meditation. Sometimes the circulating heat felt more like vibrations following the described path. Once, for a period of six months, he experienced nightly involuntary yogic postures that occurred in an orderly sequence.

In the Korean Zen tradition this same progression of sensation is reported. Thus the Korean Zen master and politician Dr. Seo informed me in 1974 that the chi energy travels up the body, especially the back, then over the top of the head to the face, finally passing down through the throat to terminate in the abdomen.

Uroboros

The *uroboros*—the serpent swallowing its own tail—is an ancient symbol. It stands for the continuity or great principle of life, the union between Heaven and Earth. Occasionally the body of this self-engulfing serpent is drawn half light and half dark, similar to the Chinese symbol of *yin-yang,* indicating both the play of polarities in nature and the reconciliation of apparent opposites. In the latter sense, the uroboros served as an important symbol in the Gnostic tradition, whose initiates aspired to a unified consciousness transcending the egoic personality and mind.

It was this archetypal symbol that the nineteenth-century German chemist Kekule saw in a dream and which gave him the idea that the molecular structure of benzene was a closed carbon ring.

In the modern esoteric school of Arica, founded by Oscar Ichazo, "the uroboros" is an exercise in which energy is generated in the lower abdomen through controlled breathing. On inhalation one focuses on the perineal area, first sensing and then directing the energy up the spine to the back of the head. Then the energy curves over the skull, and with the expired breath begins its downward path. It moves through the center of the head to the forehead where it splits at the eyes and descends along the sides of the nose and upper lip to meet again at the chin. (A similar splitting of the energy occurs according to the Korean Zen teaching, and we may also have a hidden reference to this phenomenon in the ancient Egyptian symbol of the eye of Osiris.) From the chin the energy continues down the front of the throat through the breastbone until it reaches the lower abdomen. The energy automatically travels the final distance from the abdomen to the genitals in due course. The purpose of this exercise is to "see" a light either in the head or traveling through the circuit.

Some Classical Accounts of Kundalini Arousal

Swami Narayanananda (1960), author of the first detailed book on the kundalini experience, distinguished between a *partial* and a *full* arousal of the kundalini energy. Whereas partial arousal can lead to all kinds of physical and mental complications, only the kundalini's complete ascent to the center at the crown of the head will awaken the true impulse to God-realization, or liberation, and bring about the desired revolution in consciousness. Only then can the body-mind be transcended in the unalloyed bliss of enlightenment.

The arousal of the kundalini power is accompanied by different sensations and experiences. Swami Narayanananda (1960) has compiled a list of symptoms from which the following points are taken:

1. There is a strong burning, first along the back and then over the whole body.

2. The kundalini's entrance into the central spinal canal, called *sushumna*, is attendant with pain. Swami Narayanananda makes a special point of mentioning that this and any of the other disturbing phenomena should not be taken as a sign of disease.

3. When the kundalini reaches the heart, one may experience palpitations.

4. One feels a creeping sensation from the toes, and sometimes the whole body starts to shake. The rising sensation may feel like an

ant crawling slowly up the body toward the head, or like a snake wiggling along, or a bird hopping from place to place, or like a fish darting through calm water, or like a monkey leaping to a far branch.

All these signs are mentioned in the traditional scriptures of Hinduism, notably those of Yoga and Tantrism. That in itself could be an argument for the objective nature of the kundalini process.

Saint Ramakrishna, one of modern India's greatest virtuosos of mysticism, described his kundalini experiences in strikingly similar terms. Speaking of the various ecstatic states to which he was naturally inclined, he is reported (see Nikhilananda 1942) to have said:

> In these samadhis [ecstatic states] one feels the sensation of the Spiritual Current to be like the movement of an ant, a fish, a monkey, a bird, or a serpent.
> Sometimes the Spiritual Current rises through the spine, crawling like an ant. Sometimes, in samadhi, the soul swims joyfully in the ocean of divine ecstasy, like a fish. Sometimes, when I lie down on my side, I feel the Spiritual Current pushing me like a monkey and playing with me joyfully. I remain still. That Current, like a monkey, suddenly with one jump reaches the Sahasrara [crown center]. That is why you see me jump up with a start. Sometimes, again, the Spiritual Current rises like a bird hopping from one branch to another. The place where it rests feels like fire . . . Sometimes the Spiritual Current moves up like a snake. Going in a zigzag way, at last it reaches the head and I go into samadhi. A man's spiritual consciousness is not awakened unless his Kundalini is aroused. (p. 29)

The work of another Hindu authority, Swami Vishnu Tirtha (1962), is noteworthy insofar as it builds a bridge between the classical traditions of Yoga and its modern proponents. This holy man described the signs of kundalini awakening in vivid personal terms. His description covers all the different sensory systems as well as the various motor and other manifestations.

An autobiography rich in descriptive detail is that of Swami Muktananda (1974), a master of the Indian Siddha tradition who has attracted numerous Western disciples. He reported involuntary body movements, transfixation in strange postures, strong flows of energy through the body, unusual breathing patterns, inner lights and sounds, terrifying visions and auditions (voices, sounds), and many other extraordinary mystical phenomena. He would, for instance, smell perfumes during meditation, taste nectar, and experience blisses.

But there were also unpleasant side effects. "My body was heated up and my head became heavy. Each cell of my body began to groan" (p. 61). He particularly noted that his anal area was pierced with pain. He, moreover, mentioned how he was occasionally overwhelmed by sexual desire—a confession also made, for instance, by the Sufi practitioner Irina Tweedie (1979). The connection between the stimulation of the life-force and sexual energy has been recognized by all the esoteric traditions, especially Tantrism and Taoism.

The progression of Swami Muktananda's kundalini experience, which lasted several years, finally culminated when he passed beyond all such experiences to become permanently established in "perfect peace and equanimity" (p. 163).

From a clinical standpoint, it is important to note that in the early stages of Swami Muktananda's kundalini awakening, he was often confused and fearful, having no control over the wild body movements, awkward postures, or dazzling lights in his head. Much of the time, he believed he was going insane. It is easy to imagine the diagnosis if he had approached a psychiatrist instead of his guru for help. And yet, once the initial difficulties had been overcome, he was able to function perfectly well and even to help many other people in their spiritual quest.

Another autobiography that documents a spontaneous kundalini awakening is that of Gopi Krishna (1971), a teacher and administrator in Kashmir. In addition to making many valuable self-observations, Gopi Krishna's book also includes a psychological commentary by James Hillman, who compares the kundalini experience with the Jungian model of psychosis.

Although Gopi Krishna had had psychic experiences as a child, he became an agnostic as a young man. Nevertheless, he meditated regularly for many years. He had no mystical experiences of any kind until 1937 when he was thirty-four years old. At that time he experienced a spontaneous arousal of the kundalini power that radically changed his life. From then on he remained constantly aware of his consciousness as a luminous field, waxing and waning mysteriously. Then, in 1943, he had a powerful kundalini experience leading to ecstatic unification, or samadhi. He wrote of that event:

> I distinctly felt an incomparably blissful sensation in all my nerves moving from the tips of fingers and toes and other parts of the trunk and limbs towards the spine, where, concentrated and intensified, it mounted upwards with a still more exquisitely pleasant feeling to pour into the upper region of the brain a rapturous and exhilarating stream of a rare radiating nerve secretion. In the absence of a more suitable appellation, I call it nectar . . . (p. 186)

This blissful sensation vanished when he paid attention to it, but it would flow upward with growing intensity so long as he ignored it. Suddenly, with a roar like that of a waterfall, he felt a stream of liquid light entering his brain through the spinal cord. His body began to rock, and he was enclosed in a halo of light. He became one with his surroundings and was overwhelmed with bliss.

This was followed by feelings of terror, weakness, and indifference to people. His mouth tasted bitter, his throat felt scorched, and frequently his whole body felt as if it was pierced by countless hot pins. He suffered from insomnia. In the dark he noted a reddish glow around himself. At times this was associated with severe back pains. He felt that the kundalini was operating in the wrong manner and that he might die.

Once the kundalini process had been awakened in him, Gopi Krishna was completely at its mercy. It took many years before he attained a state of physical balance and equanimity. But once the active kundalini was stabilized, it formed the basis for the gradual development of extraordinary mental gifts, creativity, and tranquillity. It also led to all kinds of mystical experiences. Early on, he experienced a dramatic expansion of his body image. "I felt as if I were looking at the world from a higher elevation than that from which I saw it before" (p. 51). He was also able to perceive his environment from all directions as it were. This experience is known as the "great body" or the "single eye."

An American Case

W. Thomas Wolfe (1978), a computer programmer, remembers how at age twelve he experienced a curious phenomenon that, in retrospect, amounted to a first kundalini awakening. At the time, he was participating in a rapid calculation contest. As the teacher was reading the first question, Wolfe felt a strange excitement and his body started to vibrate "with some inner energy" (p. 57). Then "I noticed a brightness through and about me—a light that had never been so bright before. In a way the feeling was similar to, but stronger than, the activity one feels in his midsection just before throwing up. But now it was noticeable throughout the whole body, and was a good feeling, an 'alive' feeling, rather than a sensation of sickness" (p. 57).

No sooner had his teacher finished the arithmetical question than he blurted out the answer. He had never before shown any particular aptitude for rapid calculation, and when asked to explain how he arrived at the correct answer so quickly, he was quite unable to do so. He continued to produce the right answers and won that contest and several others over the next few years.

Around the age of seventeen this mysterious ability faded. In 1974, when Wolfe started to meditate, the kundalini began to be active again. This activity was enhanced through his regular use of biofeedback. Then, at the beginning of February 1975, the following strong kundalini experience occurred:

> I had just rolled onto my back and was waiting for the oncoming slumber when I began to see a faintly pulsating light in my mind's eye . . . Shortly thereafter, an internal query was made somewhere deep within me. It was a question about whether the experience should be permitted to continue . . . The query was answered almost immediately, in the same nearly subliminal manner. The decision was to go ahead—intensify—rather than cut off the experience. All of this transpired without words.

Immediately the lights intensified and overpowered me. I could no longer quite understand the experience.

The intensification was accompanied by many strange, loud sounds—discordant, but somehow not unpleasant. These were not quite understandable either.

At the same time, I felt a strong current running between the center of my head and my forehead, terminating just above my right eyebrow. This feeling was quite pleasant—almost sexual . . .

After this period of initial confusion, the lights changed drastically. From a non-understandable pattern of random light, they snapped into an understandable, fixed, holographic pattern of large, luminous balls . . . My body-sense, with which my self had associated all my life, had changed into a "luminous-ball-sense," in which the new environment of luminous spheres was my new body. (pp. 83–84)

This kundalini awakening was followed by a spate of archetypal dreams and psychic experiences, including the ability to "transmit" or what Wolfe calls the "satsang effect." The Hindi word *satsang*, which is derived from Sanskrit *sat-sanga*, means literally "company of the truth" or "connection with the real." It generally refers to the traditional practice of sitting in the presence of an awakened or enlightened master. Such sitting in proximity to an enlightened adept is universally acknowledged as a means of spiritual awakening.

This "satsang effect," or psychic contagion, applies even in ordinary situations: We all participate in one another's psychic state, as is quickly verified when we are in the company of a sick or depressed person, which tends to drain our energy. Likewise, we are positively affected by being in the presence of a happy individual. It would appear that in the case of a person with an awakened kundalini, his or her state of being can have a still more remarkable effect on others.

Wolfe's kundalini symptoms gradually increased. Then, at the beginning of April, he experienced more classic signs of kundalini activity. He wrote:

I was startled by a forceful thrusting and thumping about in my lower back, the *Kanda* region of classical Kundalini lore. A humorous thought arose as the movement began—it felt like a squirrel thumping about to get out. It was like sitting on a living being.

Soon my stomach got very hot and I began to sweat. (p. 114)

This activity in the lower back continued over the next few days. By the end of the month, "a relentless heat—a conflagration—had begun to move slowly over the surface of my entire head" (p. 111). He heard loud noises, and pressure built up inside his skull. He continued to see lights, including the blue *bindu* ("spot") emphasized by Swami Muktananda. Next the kundalini initiated all kinds of spontaneous bodily movements (known as *kriya* in Sanskrit). A year later, Wolfe was hospitalized. He recollects: "I developed a frightening yogic symptom in mid-1976 that put me in a coronary care unit for three days. This experience was quite similar to the pseudo heart seizure of Franklin Jones [Da Love-Ananda]" (p. 125). Later he developed digestive problems.

In early 1977, Wolfe cut back on meditation and biofeedback sessions, and after a few months the unpleasant side effects of kundalini activity disappeared. When he resumed his meditation practice, he did so from a different disposition: He no longer hankered after psychic experiences or spiritual visions, realizing that no experience can ever be ultimately fulfilling. He had discovered the truth of self-transcendence.

The small self must dissolve—go away. And this is not something one can force or do. It is what remains when one just gives up and surrenders oneself to what will be.

Slowly, now, the light begins to dawn on me. My search winds down as the light of day begins to filter through the window. (p. 127)

A Visionary Experience

Flora Courtois (1970) is an American writer and Zen meditator whose "enlightenment" experience was confirmed by the famous

Zen master Yasutani Roshi. Although I know this woman personally, I am placing her in this section because her account is in print. I am citing her case here because it offers a useful contrast to Thomas Wolfe's kundalini experience, as described in the preceding section. In fact, the two accounts are so strikingly different that they afford a convenient starting point for discussing the difference between kundalini arousal and what I propose to call "visionary experience."

Courtois' first experience of the "deepest truth" came during a semiconscious state following a general anesthetic. After undergoing spontaneous unitive experiences, in which she seemed to fuse with nature, she became preoccupied with how visual perception occurs. When she wrote of her complex observations, one of her teachers thought she was mentally disturbed and sent her to a psychiatrist. This led to a short hospitalization which upset her greatly. She was so depressed over being misunderstood that she contemplated suicide. However, her suicidal thoughts ended one day when "the focus of my sight seemed to have changed; it had sharpened to an infinitely small point which moved ceaselessly in paths totally free of the old accustomed ones as if flowing from a new source" (p. 30).

Courtois then went into an ecstatic state that lasted for many days. Even though she was immersed in ecstatic bliss, her extraordinary condition in no way interfered with her daily activities. Since then she has lived a productive and happy life.

Apart from the failure to diagnose her state correctly as a spiritual experience rather than a psychopathological condition, this case is of special interest because she had few of the symptoms commonly associated with the kundalini awakening. Her adolescent experiences alone would lead one to anticipate more kundalini symptoms in her later life. But when she began Zen meditation, in 1967, she had instead only one remarkable experience.

She was sitting in the meditation hall when she saw a bright light. It seemed so real to her that she assumed the electric lights had actually been switched on. Although she realized she was still in relative darkness, she continued to see brightness for several minutes.

We have seen how the visionary experience of light, or radiance, is a frequent symptom of kundalini arousal. We can now argue that either Courtois' experience was an incomplete kundalini awakening, or it was an experience independent of the kundalini phenomenon. Gopi Krishna's (1971) argument is that all mystical experiences are based on the activation of the kundalini. Indeed, he seems to be saying that the kundalini underlies *all* experiences, since the kundalini is the motor that drives the bioenergy of the human system.

My own argument is that the physio-kundalini, which is what is being discussed here, is a particular set of experiences that is to be treated as a special case within the vast spectrum of psychic or spiritual experiences. The experiences described by Courtois belong to the nonkundalini group.

Chapter 6

CASE HISTORIES

This chapter presents seventeen case histories of kundalini arousal. I have personally interviewed fifteen of these individuals. The other two were interviewed by a colleague, though I saw one of them briefly as well. Some of these people were referred to me for their physical or psychological problems or because of their difficulties in meditation. Others I sought out after hearing of their unusual experiences. Most of them have become personal friends and have shared their experiences with me in great depth.

In all cases, my follow-up enquiries revealed a normalization of the kundalini process and its integration with the rest of the physical, emotional, and intellectual life of these individuals.

Case #1: Male Professor in the Humanities

This sixty-nine-year-old man, who had many psychic experiences as a child, awoke from a nap one day in 1963 to discover a three-inch blister on his thigh where his hand had been resting. This extraordinary experience stimulated his interest in the powers of the mind. Within two years he was meditating regularly, though without expert guidance. Then, in 1967, he began formal Zen meditation.

After a few months, during a sitting, he became engulfed by a bright golden light that lasted several minutes. He had a recurrent experience a few weeks later.

During many sittings he noticed prickling and itching sensations moving up the inside of his legs to his groin, in his arms and chest, up his back and over his head to his brows. From there the sensations moved to his cheeks, the outside of his nostrils, and sometimes to his chin. Later he experienced tingling and itching in his throat during meditation. All these symptoms point to a typical physio-kundalini cycle.

Today, ten years later and several years into his retirement, the professor no longer experiences any dramatic manifestations of the kundalini process. He is, however, able to encourage energy flows starting in his pelvis and spreading upwards. These flows, he feels, revitalize him and have even cured him of chronic lower back pain. Occasionally he feels an energy blockage in his throat, which is the precise location where the kundalini energy seemed to have been arrested when I first saw him.

Nevertheless, he reports many interesting physical changes in recent years. Doing only mild aerobic exercises, he feels ten years younger. His shoulders and chest have increased in size by several inches, while his waist has shrunk by as much. He is fifteen pounds lighter. His hands still get very hot at times. He hears sounds of bells, and sometimes he is awakened by a loud zzzing sound.

He is leading a quiet life, interrupted only by occasional visits from former students whom he counsels. He is very sensitive to the psychic dimension and frequently has precognitive dreams, usually foretelling events that occur soon after.

It would appear that regularity and discipline seem to favor a steady progression of the physio-kundalini process and its overall integration with one's psychophysical being. By contrast, a less disciplined, more freewheeling psychic orientation, emphasizing trance states, entities, and similar phenomena, tends to induce atypical kundalini activity.

Case #2: Female High School Teacher

This middle-aged teacher of Spanish has been practicing Yoga and meditation for many years. In 1980 she started to have a variety of symptoms, such as headaches, tingling in her face and nose, pains and spasms of the throat, cardiac area, and abdomen, with popping sensations all over the body. These symptoms became accentuated whenever she would meditate. She also had sensations of emptiness and of her voice not being generated by herself.

In November 1985 a dramatic change occurred. In the midst of a thirty-day meditation period, she became aware of strong flows of energy washing over her entire body. There was also a loss of sensation, except for sensory perceptions in her head. She felt the kundalini energy pushing and pulling in her face and at the top of her head. There was a bumping, jerking sensation in the cakras of the throat, the heart, and the abdomen. These sensations were predictably intensified during the most concentrated meditations. Each area also felt greatly heated up in turn. Then she started to hear machinerylike noises in her head that became continuous over the next few weeks. With her eyes closed, she could see white light streaming from her face and head.

These symptoms subsided somewhat after three months but were triggered again after a period of intense meditation and lasted for several weeks. The kundalini energy resumed its flow up the spine and down the face and trunk. She experienced great rapture and ecstatic orgasmic sensations until she began to tire of this hyperstimulation of her nervous system.

Shortly afterward she developed laryngeal spasms, which were accompanied by the fear of choking to death. Then the symptoms returned in full and for several weeks she experienced "heart attacks." As soon as these symptoms started to subside she began to suffer from sudden acute sciatica, which was clinically typical and later diagnosed by NMR scan as a ruptured disc pressing on the nerve. After three months of therapy, which did not alleviate her painful condition, she agreed to have surgery. By that time she had developed pronounced foot drop. There was intense pain extending from her lower back to her left big toe. She suffered from numbness of the sciatic distribution and great stiffness. Then, nearly as dramatically, there was a sudden subsidence of sciatica, and within three days she could walk with only a slight limp. Now, six months later, she only suffers a slight residual weakness of the lower left leg.

Her impression was that she must have had some weakness in her back that did not show until the intense kundalini energy became active in that area and precipitated the actual pathology. She looks upon her practically instantaneous healing as a gift of grace. All of her symptoms have disappeared, even though she continues to meditate.

Case #3: Female Artist-Teacher

I first saw this forty-five-year-old woman ten years ago. At the time, she had been doing automatic paintings for fourteen years. For the past two years she has been creating spontaneous paintings of her inner states, usually foreshadowing imminent experiences.

This cycle started when she blacked out during a painting session. When she regained consciousness, she found herself lying on the floor, with her body shaking violently and filling with great energy. This condition lasted for about half an hour and recurred the next night. The blast of energy and the trembling returned the following morning while she was doing her Yoga practices. It was then that she created her first spontaneous painting.

She immediately went on to the second painting in this series. All the while she was experiencing intense waves of energy and inner heat. She was also unaware of who or where she was. She began to worry about going insane. This was followed by free-floating anxiety and headaches. Then she worked on her third spontaneous painting while hallucinating patterns of force.

It was at that point that she fell apart. Depression set in, and she felt like dying. She hurt all over and cried a lot. Painting number four was created. She called it "Fractured," because it reflected her inner chaos.

Then, over a two-day period, she painted her own face with a snake encircling it. At night, on the day of completion, she awoke trembling all over. She saw a strange reddish being with an elephant face. "He" put his fingers on her forehead. Then she fell asleep again. She dreamt of painting eyes that came alive under her brush. Next morning she started work on a painting of the blue-red man. In a subsequent painting she depicted that man healing her broken head. A baby was born from that man and then grew up, which was captured in another painting.

In another crisis she did a painting of a red octopus. Then, while in an ecstatic state, she created a painting of a head super-imposed on a black head. Following this painting, she felt reborn.

Her ordeal resumed with painting number thirty-three. Over-come by a mood of depression, she felt as if she was imprisoned in a concentration camp, which is reflected in the gloomy scenes of several of her paintings. These spontaneous creations were followed by a painting of an egg with a "wavy person" emerging. At the end of this series, she felt alive and whole.

The next incident was fierce burning in her legs, which then spread into her chest and arms. She suffered hot and cold fevers and was unable to eat. She experienced pain on both sides of her head and behind her eyes as well as violent palpitations. Her blood pressure was found to be elevated.

Just prior to my interview with her, she experienced a cramping pain in her left big toe, as if a nail had been driven through it. My examination revealed a very red toenail, which was not due to bleeding. At this time she was also unnerved by a complete loss of hearing, which lasted for about an hour, and she believed she was going to die. She then consulted a physician, who found nothing wrong with her.

Since my interview, she has reported feeling a "throat opening" sensation, but also breathing difficulties and pressure in the head. These experiences and states seem to be associated with her Yoga practice and artistic creativity. Her teaching work seems to exert a stabilizing influence on her, and she admitted to feeling generally much better since taking it up.

Case #4: Female Psychologist

As a child, following a vacation spent in a religiously oriented summer camp, this middle-aged woman experienced feelings of oneness with God and Nature for about a year. As an adult she suffered several episodes of severe depression, and was hospitalized during one of these. In 1960 and 1970 respectively, she made two attempts at suicide and was unconscious for days each time.

In 1972 she was initiated into Transcendental Meditation, which helped her bear the tragedy of her daughter's premature death. It also cured her asthma. She practiced this form of meditation for about six months and then did not meditate for a similar period of time. When she resumed her meditation practice, she switched over to the Buddhist technique of *vipassana*, watching her breathing, body sensations, and thoughts.

She gradually increased the time spent in meditation. By the summer of 1974, she was meditating between three and four hours daily. It was then that she found her meditations deepening. During one of her sittings she experienced a strong feeling of disorientation, of not being located in space, which instilled some fear in her. Then, without warning, there was a sudden sharp pain at the base of her left big toe, which was quickly followed by a painful ripping sensation traveling up her leg. Then her lower pelvis and perineum felt as if they were swollen. When this sensation had spread to her waist, her torso suddenly was twisted violently to the right. (She would feel the pain in her left big toe whenever a new energy center was opening up further.)

In her abdomen she distinctly felt, "I must save all sentient beings." This was followed by a cold sensation pouring down over the crown of her head, shoulders, and arms into her chest, with the accompanying words, "I am not ready yet." All this occurred about an hour into her meditation and lasted between ten and thirty minutes.

During an intensive meditation retreat several months later, she again felt her whole body being pushed and pulled by a massive energy. Then she saw/felt a fountain of light erupting from the pelvic area into her head. At the same time she had a sense that there was a wide split in the middle of her body.

In 1975 she switched to Tibetan visualization techniques to correct what a Tibetan meditation master had diagnosed as a lopsided energy flow. She started to experience closing and opening of the energy centers of her body, without reason or order. There was also low-pitched buzzing in her head and throat during meditation and occasionally during the day. She continued to have spontaneous body movements and energy rushes and pains. However, by the end of that year she was again able to sleep three to four hours every night.

Subsequently she went to Swami Muktananda for spiritual guidance, after having seen him in dreams. He gave her a mantra and asked her to focus on her head, not her body, as in vipassana. She started to have more spontaneous body movements but the pain and fear lessened and feelings of ecstasy and bliss increased during meditation. She also experienced more tingling sensations and heat phenomena, particularly in her lower back and hands.

She began to see how there was a strong part of herself that was negative toward her own growth and spiritual maturation. But it was not until 1987 that she began to consciously work through the problems of her childhood that had proven formidable obstructions in her psyche.

In a recent follow-up interview, she reported her old kundalini headaches are persisting but the energetic disturbances have gone. She is now experiencing many spiritual connections with living and dead teachers. Psychic phenomena are occurring more frequently, and in particular she has developed the ability to heal instantly on occasion.

Case #5: Male Computer Specialist

This man is now in his mid-twenties. At age nine he suddenly developed shooting pains in his genitals and lower abdomen. When in bed at night, he would feel a strong force pushing its way down his throat. This was accompanied by perceptual distortions. A physician tentatively diagnosed hypoglycemia.

In his early teens, he and his friends experimented with hypnosis, and he discovered that he could easily dissociate from reality. One day, in his sixteenth year, while sitting quietly, he suddenly started to tremble uncontrollably, and his body became very hot. His abdominal pains returned with full force, accompanied by nausea. After a bowel movement these symptoms subsided. The next day, again while sitting quietly, he had an out-of-body experience (OBE). He had undergone a marginal OBE state when he was younger. On this occasion, however, he was able to move around the room very easily and to view his resting body very clearly. He became alarmed and by moving his arm was able to slip back into the body. For several weeks after this incident his world was collapsed and he felt he was going insane. He dissociated many times in school.

Later, during the fifth session in a Rolfing series in which his psoas muscle was being worked on, he had a strong emotional discharge, with a lot of crying and violent shaking. He felt the immediate need to ground himself. Suddenly there was a terrific energy, which felt to him like a fire hose that was being forced into his perineum and up his spine. When it reached his head there was a feeling of infinite space all around him and inside his skull. He also felt a sensation of a hole being bored into his forehead. All the while there was a display of colored lights around and inside his head. Upon the "penetration" of the forehead, he felt a great current of air rushing through the opening. This was followed by an infinite peace in infinite space.

Subsequently he suffered, as he sees it now, from the delusion that he was enlightened and that this infinite space and otherworldly focus were the only truths for him. A Zen master later told him that during that time he had been in a satori state.

At age eighteen he developed debilitating pains in his solar plexus. These were alleviated whenever he allowed his body to spontaneously assume various postures. Only later did he learn that these were yogic *asanas*. It was then that he started a program of yogic practices, including breath control, that he still follows every day for at least two hours. He was hoping all this would speed up his regaining the condition of satori. He also began to read spiritual literature.

Five years later he discovered the writings of Da Love-Ananda (Da Free John). In the midst of his study of these works he noticed a remarkable fullness in his abdomen and then his belly felt on fire for hours. To his surprise he noted that his girth had increased by four inches, without any gain in weight.

Soon afterward he became a student of Da Love-Ananda. He

began to realize that his intense yogic practice was born out of the terror of dying and an attempt to remove himself from the stresses of life. He no longer suffered from the delusion of being enlightened and also saw how he had not the slightest inclination toward surrendering the stronghold of the ego, which is the single most important precondition for enlightenment.

Then he had his first formal "sitting" with Da Love-Ananda. Upon looking at his teacher, who was seated before hundreds of people, this young man was suddenly possessed by the demonic urge to utterly destroy this being. He found it incredibly difficult to restrain himself from attempting a violent assault. While he was struggling with this irrational impulse, Da Love-Ananda made eye contact with him, and he was immediately thrust into his familiar state of blissfulness and infinity. But this time he was not alone. There was a complete merging with the teacher in an enclosure of love. This was the first time he had ever had such an ecstatic experience of being in this space of love and unity with another being. At this moment the thought arose in him, "I can't wait to tell my wife this." That very second it all stopped.

Gradually he became more open to this new relationship and learned to trust it. But time and again, he would rupture this by claiming credit for his condition. For a period he became acutely conscious of playing with his energy flows, as if he were masturbating with his nervous system. At other times he would enter into out-of-body states and immediately feel that this too was only an indulgence. He is now dealing with his residual resistances creatively, always reminding himself to return to the naturalness of the spiritual relationship with the teacher. Occasionally his old fears arise, but they are no longer as severe, and he is now more capable of allowing them while simultaneously locating within himself the bliss and equanimity that lies beyond fear.

Case #6: Female Artist

This woman, now in her late fifties, had practiced Transcendental Meditation for five years when she began to experience occasional tingling in her arms and heat in her hands. Next she was unable to sleep for days, with energy surging through her whole body. She also had several dreams of having her consciousness separated from her body. A continuous loud sound started to appear inside her head. Soon there were cramps in her big toes, followed by vibratory sensations in her legs. Overnight, her big toenails darkened, as if hit by a hammer, and eventually partially separated from the flesh. The tissue in her legs felt torn by vibratory sensations. The vibrations spread to her lower back and from there swept over her body up to her head, causing a sensation of a band around her head, just above the eyebrows. Then her head started to move spontaneously. Later her whole body would move sinuously, and her tongue would automatically press against the roof of her mouth.

Both phenomena are well known in yogic circles. The cleaving of the tongue against the palate is counted among the most secret practices of Yoga. It bears the technical designation of *khecari-mudra* or the "space-walking gesture." The "space" here is the inner space (*kha*) of consciousness. All kinds of psychic powers are attributed to yogins who have mastered this technique. In the case of this woman, the *mudra* or "gesture" of inverting the tongue occurred involuntarily.

She would also sense a strong sounding of "om"—the most sacred syllable in the Hindu tradition—emanating from within her head. The tingling sensations spread to her neck, upward over the head, down to the forehead and face. Both nostrils were stimulated, causing a feeling of elongation of the nose. At times her eyes seemed to move separately, and the pupils felt like holes that bored into her head and met in the center. Then she felt tremendous pressure at the back of her head, at the crown, and across the forehead. This pressure would become especially severe during reading, resulting in acute discomfort around the eyes and in a pulsing sensation at the top of the head.

This was followed by the experience of a brilliant light and of bliss and laughter.

The tingling sensation spread further down to the mouth and chin. It was then that she began to have dreams of heavenly music. Then the sensations traveled to her throat, chest, and abdomen, and eventually she felt as if there was a closing of the circuit in the shape of an egg: The energy was moving up through the spine and down through the front of the body. As it developed, the circuit activated particular energy centers on its way—starting in the lower abdomen and proceeding to the navel, the solar plexus, the heart, the head, and finally the throat. After this closure she experienced a continuous feeling of energy pouring into her body through the navel area. This feeling stopped after the circuit was completed. The whole experience had strong sexual overtones. It was also accompanied by spontaneous yogic breathing (faint and controlled).

The greater part of this kundalini activity occurred over several months. Subsequently she experienced only occasional kundalini phenomena, mostly during meditation or when relaxing in bed. Throughout the protracted experience, this woman understood that she was undergoing a kundalini awakening, since she had read about this phenomenon before. In the beginning she felt relaxed about what was happening to her and simply allowed the process to unfold as it might. But eventually she became perturbed and had difficulty integrating her experiences with her daily activities. The inflow of energy prevented normal sleep for months, and, since it continued during the day as well, she found herself incapable of efficient work. She felt herself thrown into the position of a detached observer of her own activities. In due course she brought the situation under control.

The general effect of this kundalini arousal was positive. There has been steady progress toward an ever greater sense of connectedness with what this woman calls her "higher self"—a sense of being in touch with an unshakeable core, a center, that is unaffected by all the ups and downs of everyday life. In my follow-up interview with her, she remarked: "From that core comes guidance, peace, and a sense of being in touch with, and understanding of, the essence of things 'as they are.' It also gives a sense of oneness with all life, and from that comes a love and a joy of existence. Life becomes a path of daily 'miracles' of harmony, which is expressed in synchronicities, and a feeling of trust and security in an unfailing guidance. I feel in touch with myself and the Source of all things."

She also noted that, with the exception of pressure in the head, all physical sensations have ceased.

Case #7: Male Scientist

This person, now in his sixties, began Transcendental Meditation in 1967. After about five years he suddenly started to have gross thrashing body movements during meditation and at night in bed. After a few weeks these involuntary movements subsided. Several months later, on going to bed, he felt a tingling sensation in his lower legs, followed by cramping in his big toes. The cramping extended to other muscles before it gradually faded. The tingling sensation spread to his lower back, and he "saw" a reddish light there. The light solidified into a rod, which he then sensed and "saw" being pushed up his spine. Next it extended forward to the umbilical area, accompanied by many tingling, vibrating sensations. Step by step it moved up the spine to the level of the heart and then extended forward to stimulate the cardiac plexus.

When it reached his head, he "saw" floods of white light, as if his skull were lit up from inside. Then the light seemed to spout out the top of his head as a solid beam. Some time later he felt a vibration in his right arm and wrist and also in his left leg. As soon as he attended to these sensations, they disappeared. He also experienced energy currents running through his shoulders and arms in waves of three or four per second, later increasing to seven and more per second. At one time, when he focused on the center in his head, violent and uncontrollable spasms occurred.

At various times this kundalini activity was accompanied by a variety of internal sounds, mostly high-pitched whistling and hissing. At other times, he heard flutelike musical tones. Frequently he would experience peace and bliss.

Then his sleep began to be disturbed again by automatic movements of the body. Sometimes he would awaken to find himself doing spontaneous yogic breathing and assuming a variety of Hatha Yoga postures. After several nights of this, the tingling sensation traveled to his forehead, nostrils, cheeks, mouth, and chin. This whole process was accompanied by ecstatic feelings, and he experienced sexual arousal when the activity centered in the pelvic area. Then all these effects ceased, returning only from time to time when he relaxed at night in bed, and he could shut these off by turning on his side.

About a year later, pressure developed in his head at night and started to move downward. Simultaneously, a tingling sensation moved upward from his stomach. He experienced all this activity as if from a distance. The two stimuli met at the throat, and he felt as if a hole appeared where they joined. He further experienced, still from a detached witnessing disposition, all manner of purely spontaneous sounds being emitted from that hole in the throat. Approximately six months later, the stimulus moved down from the throat to the abdomen, where it remained for a few months before moving further down into the pelvic area.

This scientist had an inherently sensitive nervous system. Yet his awareness that he was undergoing a kundalini arousal and his knowledge of what to expect, together with the stabilizing effect of a meditative discipline, made him less susceptible to the disorganizing aspects of the kundalini cycle. He realized that whatever difficulties he did encounter were the result of overstrenuous meditation practice, and so he was not beset by anxiety during the process.

Case #8: Actress

This woman, now in her early forties, had many psychic experiences in her childhood. As an adolescent she suffered from recurring migraine headaches, mental disorganization, and impulsive disruptive behavior. She received psychotherapy for these symptoms for several years, was diagnosed schizophrenic, but was never hospitalized. When she was twenty-four years old she began to meditate, using various techniques. About a year later, her headaches became worse. But then, within a few weeks, her head pains, mental disorganization, and disruptive behavior suddenly ceased.

Within a year, tingling sensations started in her legs, then spread to her arms and chest. After a few weeks they extended to her neck and the back of her head, and soon down to her forehead. They were more noticeable during meditation. At intervals her entire body, but especially her hands, would become very hot. During meditation she was also troubled by swaying and jerking of her body, and by anxiety.

In fact, she came to my attention because of the severity of her anxiety and the violence of the automatic movements during meditation. I advised her to discontinue her self-styled meditation and take up some established meditative practice. Until this was possible, I suggested that she temporarily decrease her sensitivity to the kundalini process by discontinuing her periodic fasting and strict vegetarian diet. Once she was supervised in her practice of Transcendental Meditation, all disturbing symptoms soon ceased.

Sometime later the physio-kundalini cycle started again. During one long meditation she became aware of her throat in a new way. She felt as if her head had become separated and floated above her trunk; her throat started to produce sounds on its own, and she became aware of a separate observer-self. Most of her kundalini symptoms ceased after this experience, which was a typical "throat opening."

Since then her meditations have been quiet and peaceful. She reports that her productivity and contentment have greatly increased. It is my conjecture that many psychosislike aspects of her personality were simply due to the fact that she had for so many years failed to find a useful outlet for her psychic energies.

In this connection it is helpful to recall the experience of the British psychic Matthew Manning (1975), who was plagued by poltergeist phenomena from an early age. These persisted until he discovered that he could do automatic writing. Soon he found that he could paint in the style of several great painters, completing a work in ten to twenty minutes. This then turned out to be his most fruitful channel of expression. Once the bulk of his energy could be thus expressed, the poltergeist activities ceased.

It may be that in child prodigies it is their very specialization, or talent, that stabilizes them early in life. They experience fewer conflicts than an individual with a surplus of psychic energy but no appropriate channel for conducting it. Child psychics may have it difficult from the start because of the disturbing and disruptive nature of their genius. Genuine spirituality seldom emerges as early as other talents. Even such spiritual adepts as Jesus of Nazareth, Gautama the Buddha, the South Indian sage Ramana Maharshi, and the contemporary American master Da Love-Ananda (Da Free John) did not enjoy the fullness of their enlightenment until puberty or later.

Creativity, whether it be of a great writer, musician, poet, painter, or dancer, does not seem to favor the kind of change in the nervous system that is associated with the kundalini arousal. Perhaps their creative work grounds them more, or possibly there are fewer blocks in the nervous system when genius is narrowly channeled, and so changes in the nervous system may occur without the dramatic signs of the physio-kundalini cycle. I also tentatively suggest that the creative activity of such geniuses may spring from a more subtly functioning area of the nervous system than is indicated by the manifestations of the physio-kundalini. Finally, I wish to suggest that the central nervous system must be relatively mature for the physio-kundalini process to occur at all.

Case #9: Female Psychologist

In 1973 this woman, then in her forty-first year, noted the onset of heat in her head and chest, with tingling sensations over her body and head during meditation. She had been engaged in various intensive group and meditation disciplines for a number of years. Another curious phenomenon occurred during that time. Whenever she would do the tongue-and-palate exercise she had been taught during a meditation retreat, she would experience orgasmlike waves rippling through her body.

She felt hot much of the time, particularly in her chest and throat, yet sensations of coldness were mixed in. She felt shaped like an egg, and her whole being felt unified. Vibrations started in the pelvic area and from there moved up her back to her neck. Her chest felt soft and open. She heard brilliant bird song inside her head and felt a tingling in her throat. Once, three years earlier, she had felt like a giant heart while meditating. At the time, she experienced a prickly itching heat all over her body, but she was not troubled because she believed that these sensations indicated successful and centered meditations and a flow between herself and others. She assumed that she was experiencing a kundalini awakening, which she believed to be dangerous unless the "higher mind" was in control.

A few months after the kundalini symptoms started in 1973, she felt, during meditation, as if she were two feet taller than her normal self and as if her eyes were looking out from above her head. At this time she was sure that she knew what people were thinking, and many of her impressions were confirmed.

Soon after this, her feet began to hurt and headaches started. The headaches grew worse whenever she attempted to stop the rippling sensations she was experiencing in her body. She noted that the headaches came when she tried to regulate the rush of energy passing through her. Massage helped the pain in her feet, but it was still so severe that she could walk only with difficulty and was unable to drive. She ate very little, her sleep was fitful, and she suffered some nausea. It was hard for her to talk with people. At times, she questioned the reality of her experiences, wondering if they were just a crazy episode.

She felt heat on one side of her back and was convinced that, unless it spread to both sides, she would be in danger. Once she succeeded in spreading it, this crisis passed. Then a tingling sensation started to move from her pelvis up her back and to her neck. She began to see light inside her skull. She was amazed to find that she could see this light all the way down her spine as well. The energy and tingling moved over her forehead and became focused under her chin. She felt as if there were a hole in the top of her head. Sleep became very difficult for her, and for the next six weeks, meditation was the only thing that helped her. She felt that if she did not meditate, the heat flowing in her body would grow so intense as to damage her system. Other people could feel excessive heat when they touched her lower back.

Although she felt "strange" at times, she was determined to avoid psychiatric help during her trouble, because she feared that she would be labeled and treated as insane. When her symptoms were more than she could bear alone, she worked with various meditation teachers.

Then she began to experience rippling sensations and shaking of her body, and she felt as though she was being cleansed and balanced. Shortly afterward, she felt a prickling in her cheeks and under her chin. Then all unpleasant phenomena ceased, and she had no further difficulty, although she continued her meditation practice. She underwent this physio-kundalini cycle in the span of a year. She later started a successful center for personal growth and was able to help others who experienced difficulties in the kundalini process.

Her many distressing physical problems were probably due to residual blocks and unresolved conflicts that were locked into her body. These would presumably not have caused her any significant emotional or physical difficulties had her kundalini remained inactive.

For the past decade or so, this woman has worked as a therapist. Healing has become an integral part of her practice physically, psychologically, and spiritually. During sessions with her patients, she is able to tune into their feelings, physical condition, and personal images. The energetic manifestations have continued almost constantly, and they tend to increase when she devotes more time to meditation.

As her mind becomes quiet and the silence deepens, there is a heightened awareness and perception. Her whole being begins to vibrate and is "charged with the energy of awareness." The vibrations occur horizontally and vertically, and when they are at their most intense they cause a slight tremor in her hands. Over the years, this state of awareness has increased in intensity and duration. It is accompanied by the sensation of heat in the lumbar region, which rises and spreads to the top of her head. During these periods of inner silence, she is able to perceive a variety of sounds and colors in her body.

There is no inner dialogue but, if called upon to speak, there is great precision of language that is much more directly satisfying than her usual speech. "The challenge is to move in and out of the silence with greater ease and fluidity, and to be comfortable and confident in various social situations—both professionally and personally." During these sensitive states, which can continue for several days at a time, she experiences openness, freedom, compassion, truth, calmness, joy, and love.

Case #10: Female Librarian

This woman, now in her mid-fifties, had been a meditator in her own style for many years. One day, in 1968, she lost awareness while meditating with her hands on a table. She awoke to find char marks on the table corresponding to her hand prints. She had the table refinished before I could examine it. No heat manifestation of this kind ever happened again. Because she did not show a regular progression of symptoms, I regarded her as a possible case of arrested physio-kundalini.

In 1969 she acquired a "psychic guide," which she found very useful in her daily life. Three years later she became involved in the study of the dreams and drawings of children and even completed an impressive manuscript on this theme. With this newfound interest, the intervention of her guide has ceased.

Case #11: Male Writer-Psychic

This forty-year-old, who is a productive writer and successful wood sculptor, had been meditating for two years when he began to experience heat sensations. During one such episode he took his oral temperature with an electronic thermometer: It read 101 degrees Fahrenheit, but dropped within a minute or two to 99 degrees. A short time later, his hand temperature was 104 degrees. He was not ill.

Around the same time, he started to experience spontaneous trance states. During these he would receive information psychically, some of which was confirmed. He came to my attention because of marital difficulties brought on by his trance states. I encouraged him to learn to enter a light trance at will, and his spontaneous trance states stopped.

The physical signs of this man were similar to those of the preceding two cases. His personality and orientation were similar to those of the librarian. He made no connections to traditional methods of meditation, though he did study briefly with a curandero healer not unlike Carlos Castaneda's (1968) Don Juan. He was more attracted to psychic phenomena and powers than to what C. G. Jung called the "inner dialogue." This may partially explain his being overpowered by trance states. Jung has repeatedly emphasized that, unless hidden inner drives are somehow dealt with in dreams or through some form of inner dialogue, they will manifest obliquely, in autonomous ways that can cause emotional and physical difficulties.

Case #12: Male Artist-Healer

This man, now in his late thirties, remembers his earliest psychic experiences as being lucid dreams in childhood. During one such dream, he saw his "double" pick up the bed clothes, which had fallen off, and hand them to him. He was frightened by the vividness of the experience.

Aged twenty-two, he began to practice Transcendental Meditation. He had many insights and achieved much tension release. But then he made such rapid progress in meditation that, lacking proper guidance, he started to have anxiety attacks during his sittings. Once he had a vision of white light and lost consciousness. Just preceding this vision, he experienced a flow of energy that started in his abdomen and proceeded to his back, up to his neck, and then to the back of his head, where it burst into brilliant light. He also felt heat in his abdomen and head.

Subsequently, hissing and roaring sounds occurred during his meditations. As his anxiety grew worse, he shifted to Zen meditation and found some relief. Then he experienced another vision of white light. Next he went abroad with his family, visiting several psychic healers. He had "psychic surgery" for lifelong migraine headaches and since then has had no recurrences. Members of his family were likewise healed of a number of chronic disorders.

He was so impressed with psychic healing that he returned to film one of the healers. Shortly before his return he began to have precognitive visions. In the end he decided to apprentice with one of the healers. For two years he learned all he could about psychic healing and found that he became more and more successful at it. He would experience energy flows and clairvoyantly sense a person's malady, healing friends and acquaintances whenever the opportunity presented itself. His artistic work started to flourish.

At first he was quite unsure of his newly acquired abilities. His old anxiety returned for a while, but subsided when he saw several persons recover from serious illnesses after his healing work with them. Throughout this time he continued to practice meditation, and he would occasionally experience some tingling in his cheeks and along both sides of his nose.

Case #13: Male Engineer-Healer

This former aeronautical engineer, now in his sixties, has been a meditator and healer for many years. In 1973 he suddenly began to have unusual body sensations. He felt pressure in his head, followed by a week of insomnia. Then the pressure changed to vibratory sensations, and he felt heat in his body. As the vibrations spread from his head to his shoulders, and chest, and down into his legs, he felt as if his body would explode. When these sensations peaked, the back of his tongue would often develop blisters.

He experienced waves of colored light pouring through his head and body, and the light would turn golden as it spread. After three weeks of this he felt washed clean and found that he could control most of the sensations through meditation. He believes that his healing abilities have increased as a result of these experiences, which was confirmed by my inquiries of his clients.

These two healers illustrate extremes of self-discipline. Whereas the younger man apprenticed himself to a mature healer, the older man pursued his discipline in a solitary setting. Every night for five years he would awake early to meditate for two hours. He trained himself to sleep instantly at the end of each session, and he learned to separate his consciousness the moment he lay down. Their approaches were also quite distinct. The younger man used an intuitive method in a setting that fully evoked his instincts; the engineer-healer applied a great deal of will and one-pointed effort.

I saw this application of will in another case—that of a successful psychic. I tested this man with magnetic stimulation of his right brain, using the method described by Bentov in his seminal essay included in this volume. For some time following the experiment, which involved exposure of the right cerebral hemisphere to a pulsating magnetic field, this person found that he could visualize colors only in the blue-green part of the spectrum, and that his word flow was impaired. The problem with language cleared in a few days, but color visualization took an additional week to be fully restored. He also experienced some stiffness in his neck, which disappeared when the ability to visualize all colors returned.

I believe that this man predominantly used his will to achieve psychic effects, showing a dominance of the left cerebral hemisphere. His inherent sensitivity permitted him to respond to the new kind of cerebral activity initiated by the experiment. The new activity of the right brain then came into competition with the usual, well-controlled state in which the left brain was dominant. This may explain the initial left-sided symptoms. The temporary state of confusion lasted until his accustomed homeostasis was reestablished.

Case #14: Female Secretary

This woman had been practicing Transcendental Meditation for two years when, early in 1975, she began to have tingling and numbness in her lower legs. She was twenty-eight years old at the time. Soon stiffness in one leg began to interfere with walking. She consulted several doctors, including neurologists. When myelographic studies (X-rays of the spine after the injection of radio-opaque oil) were suggested, she refused. It occurred to her that her symptoms were worse after days of prolonged meditations, and so she decided to seek advice about the effects of her meditative practice instead.

It looked likely that she was in the early stages of the physio-kundalini cycle, and that the stress and worry about possible physical disease were increasing her difficulties. I was able to reassure her that her symptoms were part of a normal process in the nervous system that was proceeding too rapidly because of her

excessive practice of meditation. Reassurance and temporary cessa-
tion of meditation soon had her on the road to recovery. Later she
resumed her meditative practice—in moderation. The physio-
kundalini cycle continued to unfold without undue side effects.

Case #15: Housewife

This woman, now in her late thirties, began Transcendental Meditation in the mid-70s. She quickly developed tingling and occasional
stocking-type numbness in her left foot and leg. When her mother-
in-law moved into the house with her and her husband, the
symptoms grew worse; she got a stiff leg and developed foot drop.
She went for medical help, and a myelogram was done. Subsequently the symptoms increased, and she was put on cortisone.
She was told by her neurologist that she might never recover full use
of her leg. This severely depressed her, and she became almost
nonfunctional. It was at this time that she came to my attention.

This woman had an extraordinarily sensitive nervous system,
and was clearly in the early stages of the physio-kundalini cycle. Her
worry about the prognosis and the effect of the cortisone treatment
had led to pain and stiffness in her back and legs. Once her
symptoms were correctly identified as resulting from an awakened
kundalini, her full recovery was guaranteed. Today, with ten more
years of experience with similar cases, I would say that some slight
residual impairment of function is not unusual.

Case #16: Housewife

In 1972 this woman, who was then in her mid-fifties, experienced
the onset of an intense and disturbing process. She suddenly felt that
something was descending over her head. Indira Devi (see Roy and
Devi 1974) described in almost identical words this experience,
which happened during her first meditation and which was soon
followed by a spontaneous kundalini awakening. In the case of our
woman, this feeling or sensation was followed by a fainting spell.

This pattern recurred several times. Remarkably, she was never groggy after regaining awareness, as might be expected with a convulsive disorder. Physicians were unable to give her any relief.

Then, one time, she heard a voice saying inside her head: "Are you ready?" Later she heard internal music. One day she was feeling well until late in the afternoon when the base of her left big toe started to ache. Soon the pain extended up her shin, and she could feel the workings of her knee joint. The pain was intermittent but disabling. She spent a few days in bed, where she spontaneously assumed many yogic poses.

Several days later, her body felt "worked on" from the toes up the back in segments. This process was accompanied by pain on both sides of her nose and by waves of energy and tingling sensations up her neck and down her face. There was also the sensation of intense heat in her back, and she experienced severe viselike pressure around her head. During some of these energy flows she was forced to breathe in a sighing manner. Occasionally there were torsional whipping movements of her head and neck, and once the energy moved down into her head, causing her scalp to get cold and her face to get hot.

Over a period of about three years, she slowly became convinced that she had been selected by God to be born anew as an advanced human being. Thus she yielded to the tendency that Jung (1975) had warned against: that of claiming this impersonal force as her own ego creation and, as a result, of falling into the trap of ego inflation and false superiority. She expected others to understand exactly what she was speaking about and to accept her word unquestioningly, and she grew distrustful of anyone who disagreed with her interpretations. This woman has never submitted to the discipline of regular meditation, and was also not interested in any help I had to offer.

Case #17: Male Psychiatrist

This colleague of mine, now in his early forties, had been meditating regularly for three years and also had served as a subject in our research with the magnetic stimulator when, in 1975, he experienced a kundalini awakening. It is worth noting that he was born with a spinal defect for which he had surgery that left him with chronic lower back pain since his teens.

In December 1975 this psychiatrist attended a weekend at the school of the late Swami Muktananda in Oakland, California. Upon being touched by the Swami, he went into a deep meditation. Within ten minutes, his mouth automatically opened widely, and his tongue protruded. After a few minutes, he experienced a blissful calm and many inner visions, in which Swami Muktananda appeared to him and helped him experience a fusion with the guru. A few minutes later, he "saw" the interior of his abdomen, chest, and throat light up with a golden energy. Then his lower back began to ache severely. At the onset of the pain, a white light in his head became more and more intense. The back pain disappeared toward the end of the meditation and did not return.

Following this remarkable experience, his meditations at home became very productive. Emotional problems and unfinished incidents seemed to find solutions very rapdily and at great depth during his meditations.

Then, in the middle of January 1976, he developed a rash that formed a curved line. It began at his lower back, crossed his spine twice, and veered off to his left shoulder. He was wondering whether it might have a symbolic significance, rather like the stigmata of some Christian mystics. At about this time, he also noticed a return of the high-pitched sounds and scratching noises during meditation that he had experienced earlier, after being stimulated many times over a period of several months with the magnetic device.

In January he participated in a second weekend intensive during which he was again touched by Swami Muktananda. Immediately he felt painful tingling and hot and cold sensations spreading over his upper back and neck. His throat burned, and there were automatic movements of head and neck. Then he felt inner peace and blissfulness. Later his head started to spin, and he felt vibrations in his hands. Next his knees began to burn, and he felt a buzzing up his spine that ended in feelings of light and energy in his head. Throughout these experiences his breathing was irregular—at times rapid and shallow, at other times slow and deep. Everything seemed to be breaking loose inside him, and he felt as though he were in labor.

Toward the end of this meditation, he experienced great inner peace and a deep knowing of his inmost self, followed by a total sense of freedom and of "coming home." The next day he had difficulty returning to his usual state. He was uncoordinated and unable to concentrate. For several days he felt physically exhausted.

His meditation, however, continued to deepen. Then, for a few days, he experienced intense pain in his left big toe and left foot, which spread to his lower leg. He also had an ache on the left side of the back of his head. The pain extended to his left eye, which would occasionally close automatically. After a few days, this intermittent pain disappeared. The pain in his leg, which had resisted all treatment, cleared at about the same time.

In his day-to-day life, family and friends experienced him as more relaxed. A physical therapist, whom he saw regularly, confirmed that my friend felt more relaxed and integrated since this kundalini awakening. His sense of having "come home" grew into a feeling of at-oneness with the world.

Then, during meditation, itching developed on his forehead and occasionally on his cheeks, indicating a further progression of the physio-kundalini cycle.

Toward the end of 1976, he visited Swami Muktananda's hermitage in Ganeshpuri, India. He meditated three times a day for a total of four hours. Another two to three hours were spent chanting. During most of his meditations he experienced ecstatic love-bliss, and he would frequently "merge into the blue light of consciousness." This intense spiritual discipline stimulated the kundalini energy in the region of the first and second cakras. As a result he experienced powerful surges of energy that sent his uro-genital system into orgiastic spasms. He felt his semen flow upward through the body's central channel (traditionally known as *sushumna-nadi*).

He later understood that this experience was associated with the "piercing of the first knot." He spontaneously entered a period of complete celibacy. He witnessed the baby toenails on both his feet falling off the same night.

After his return from India, he spent several years integrating his spiritual experiences with the practicalities of daily life, achieving a rare attunement and balance. Other meditative experiences followed, indicating the "piercing of the second knot." During one of his evening meditations, back again at the Ganeshpuri ashram, the kundalini energy became intensely focused in the subtle center between the eyebrows. Swami Muktananda spontaneously walked over to him and immediately began to work his fingers over the space between the sixth center and the center at the crown of the head. Streams of kundalini energy started to flow in a V-shaped pattern toward the crown center. Since that time, he reports, the kundalini energy has rarely left the crown center.

Discussion

The physio-kundalini complex has a number of characteristic features, both objective and subjective. The typical physio-kundalini progression, as outlined, rarely occurs in practice, but often several of the effects do manifest.

If we accept the view that these effects are the results of the balancing action of the kundalini as it removes blockages throughout the system, then individual differences in symptom patterns mean that different areas are blocked. This may be due to dissimilarities in the genetic makeup and the past history of each individual. Also, the varying time involved in the unfolding of the physio-kundalini cycle—lasting from a few months to several years—may be caused by variation in the intensity of a person's meditation practice and by the total amount of balancing needed.

Often the cycle does not run its full course, as already noted. This arrest of the physio-kundalini cycle may occur in those who become fascinated with some particular psychic ability. Furthermore, the signs and symptoms are not present continuously but appear at intervals, most often during meditation, quiet time, or sleep.

Chapter 7

SELF-REPORTS

Female Artist-Writer

This highly creative woman, now in her mid-forties, lives a very productive life and has a strong desire to integrate all aspects of her life. Her kundalini activity has thus far consisted chiefly of visionary and auditory experiences, though she has also encountered other typical kundalini phenomena. The following is a summary description of her kundalini experience in her own words.

In the spring of 1966 I was awakened with such a quantum leap of subtle energy in my body that I was unable to sleep for over two months. During the following six months sleep continued to be difficult for me. At the inception of the awakening, I saw a vision of the whole earth and heard a voice saying, "Learn the deep archetypes of humanity."

It took me some time before I could really learn, study, or do anything, because my whole being was opening up into realms wholly new to me. I walked and studied at night and performed my earthly tasks of being a mother and housewife during the day.

I knew nothing about the kundalini at the time. It was others who subsequently recognized what was happening to me as a kundalini awakening. My experience was sudden, unexpected, and undeniable. It wasn't easy—all the more so since no one around me knew of such things. Though the power of the experience was not easy to endure, I often felt expanded, joyful, and extremely nourished spiritually, especially when I was alone.

In 1963 I had started Zen meditation, and I believe it was largely my meditation practice that led to the awakening. It has also been Zen and vipassana meditation that have helped me to integrate the kundalini experience.

Access to this energy is the greatest wealth of my life. Yet like all wealth it is not always easy to manage. At times, I have felt tingling energy all over my body. Sometimes I experienced it as pain, at other times as ecstasy, bliss, extreme happiness, and insight. I learned that resistance led to pain, whereas acceptance led to bliss. Gradually I learned to respond rightly. During the first two months, I came to believe that I would never sleep again. At first this was completely unacceptable to me, but eventually I came to terms with it.

Although I accepted the unacceptable, I still had no orientation, no forms or modes of life for this quantum leap in energy level. It seemed beyond my capacity. I was experiencing light and subtle realms simultaneously with ordinary sensory perception. This was very disorienting, and I sought out maps for this new territory. This was the "call" to learn the archetypes of humanity.

Eventually I began to find my questions mirrored in world myths, sacred art, religions, and mysticism, which I studied at night. The intensity of my study and quest lasted eight years. Then I finally felt that the sudden awakening of 1966 had become integrated with the rest of my life. Since then I have felt that the increase of subtle energy has been in smaller increments such that I could master it more easily, especially through meditation practice.

The spiritual cosmologies in myths, religions, and sacred art provided some clues about universal laws that included the super-sensible realms to which I had acquired access. My quest has never stopped, but in the meantime I have discovered some holistic patterns of the archetypes. This holistic orientation is, in my view, the foundation for a new life and culture.

I feel that the kundalini experience is not simply physiological or psychological but also cosmological and spiritual. In my case, it is a response to a spiritual call that demands cosmo-psychological answers. Insight into the cosmic order is synchronous with insight into the deepest levels of human nature. The kundalini energy has the voltage, or charge, that propelled me into realms that go far beyond my sensory awareness. Over the years, these supersensible realms have become the nourishment and guidance of my life.

In 1976 I again experienced a quantum leap in energy and received a vision that has been a directive in my life ever since. This vision was in regard to a universal language. At first, in my meditation, there appeared a point of intense, unearthly, beautiful blue light. Then the blue light enveloped me, and I went into a realm where I saw three immortal beings more clearly and purely than is possible in sensory perception. The central being was white, and on either side were Immortals in red and blue. An elixir dropped from the roof of my mouth (from my brain?) and pervaded my body with bliss. I saw celestial landscapes and the Immortals showed me the luminous structure behind nature. I was granted a vision of the future of our planet. I was told that there would be human travail, but that there would also be children who will understand the universal language that I was shown.

Such visions and voices are not mere hallucinations. In my understanding, the difference between visions and hallucinations lies in the fact that visions are clear directives of life, the test of which is whether they become manifest in a positive way in one's life. Hallucinations are the same psychological function, but manifest in persons who have not integrated this primal energy. It blows them apart instead.

In 1984 I experienced another quantum increase of subtle energy, accompanied by visions and voices. At that time, I saw people's cakras, auras, and many spirit beings. I learned certain shamanic techniques to work with this energy so that I could access the subtle realms and see visions and hear voices at will. It has taken me two years, however, to learn not to be caught up in the ecstasy of the energy and to ground, deepen, and integrate it.

In 1986 I fell ill because of an imbalance of the spiritual energy, which was burning me up. During the illness I realized that if I did not learn to master the subtle energy, I would live at most only five more years. Since I feel I cannot fulfill my destiny in that span of time, I am consciously working on rebuilding my physical body to sustain the increasing subtle energy.

Male Psychiatrist

This middle-aged man is a practicing Jungian analyst in whom the kundalini process was triggered through body work. Here is his account of his encounter with this great force.

Following medical school in the late 1950s, I embarked upon a psychiatric career that was first channeled through a conservative, mostly Freudian residency. Next followed six years of personal psychoanalysis. During this time I accepted reductive interpretations of numerous religious dreams as well as what I later discovered to be bona fide telepathic dreams, which intruded into my analyst's personal life. These latter dreams created some unsettling moments in this overly rational analysis.

During the final year of this analysis, C. G. Jung began appearing in my dreams, and I soon discovered his three-dimensional view of the psyche.

Once solidly engaged in my personal Jungian analysis and in training as a candidate at the local Jungian Institute, my dreams began beckoning me to explore the realm of body awareness.

My entrance into this work was accompanied by great skepticism. I had shunned readings and discussions in this area. Still influenced by the dogmatic pronouncements of one of my professors that Wilhelm Reich's writing on the armoring of the body occurred during his psychotic phase, I was very wary. Yoga and other Eastern practices and philosophies were likewise suspect to me, and I had never paid any serious attention to them.

Utter surprise overtook me about six months into this body work (which consisted in deep breathing and extremely slow movements of small segments of the body) when the areas around my eyes started convulsive-like activities. After each bout of this automatic muscular activity, I experienced a gentle vibratory sensation that grew more intense and pleasurable as time passed.

Gradually section after section of my body underwent similar movements, with the throat area being the last affected.

The pleasurable vibrating sensations gradually increased, and it took time to develop my tolerance for this pleasure. But there were also painful experiences. For several months intense heat radiated from my abdomen making it too uncomfortable for my partner to sleep close to me. When the vibrations began entering my head, I suffered three months of headaches and fears that I would become psychotic.

Over the course of seven years, these totally autonomous vibrations gradually came under the control of my ego. Presently I can tune in to the vibrations simply by closing my eyes and by directing the energy into any energy center, or cakra, desired. Numerous benefits have accrued through this long process. I am able to experience total bodily pleasure, which is in fact a meditation experience. I can free myself from stress almost immediately, distract myself from physical pain, and recharge my energy supply when depleted.

In the beginning, when the energy in my head provided me with a wonderful high, I would overindulge and find myself with a hangover effect the next day. Greed in this area also extracts a price—a refractory period of dysphoria.

My dreams often gave me directions on how to use the energy and they also warned me about dangerous pitfalls ahead. I was fortunate to be in analysis with an analyst who understood this process and the symbolic dream material.

During some of these periods of intensive energy activity, several patients reported similar activities in their own bodies in my presence.

Reflecting on the twelve years since my first experience of this inner energy, I feel I have been blessed to have experienced the unfolding and constant refinement of the kundalini force in my life. In the most uncanny ways I find myself attracted to strangers who, I discover afterward, have undergone profound body awareness work that has opened them up to a deeper spiritual awakening and a more meaningful life. I have the sense that this process is ongoing and I await further developments.

Female Health Care Professional

This single woman, who is now in her mid-thirties, triggered the kundalini in 1970 by taking LSD. At the time she had no under-standing of what was happening to her, and the symptoms associ-ated with the kundalini arousal greatly disturbed her. In March 1981, after reading the first edition of my book, she wrote to me in some detail about her history with this phenomenon. The following is an edited version of her articulate account.

My experience with kundalini was and perhaps still is the most impactive event of my life. For years I read anything I could get my hands on that might be related to my strange and at times terrifying experiences. After eleven years it is really satisfying to find your book, which synthesizes the various aspects of kundalini in a way that echoes my own conclusions.

In 1970, at the age of eighteen, I took three trips on LSD. The first two trips were beautiful and "spiritual"—during the second I experienced what was probably a form of "satori." During the third I experienced what I now call "kundalini."

Preceding the kundalini was an "awareness" of my capacity to turn off my mind and self—to annihilate my individuality without physical death. (Right now this is meaningless to me, but it was my experience.) Shortly thereafter I felt a rush—a roar—of white light shoot up from the base of my spine through and out the top of my head. I was terrified, panicked, and thought I was dying. I "yanked" down the rush of light energy. It occurred again and again, with seconds or minutes in between. I kept yanking it down. I went to an emergency room and was given thorazine. I saw a psychiatrist for six weeks. He was not very helpful but served as an anchor in my confusion.

The roar and rush of white light continued. We called this LSD flashbacks. At first it occurred several times a day. At times I would jump up from a sound sleep with the white roar. During this time I was mostly preoccupied with the certainty that I was either dying or going crazy. I was not particularly interested in the experience itself, only in stopping it. After six months of anxiety, palpitations, weight loss, and diarrhea, I went into the hospital (medical, not psychiatric) for a week of tests, and rest and recuperation. The first night I was there I closed my eyes to go to sleep and felt a light touch between my eyebrows and felt that things would now get better. I recall that during my stay I sometimes played with my hands, forming what I now know as *mudras* [spontaneous gestures]. I also remember playing at reading palms and getting tired of all the nurses who dropped in because they had heard I did this. Maybe I was good at it; I don't remember.

I started writing poetry around this time. (The only piece I ever submitted was accepted for publication.) My sketching also improved.

The next two years were difficult, even though I became more adept at controlling the energy rushes. I learned to stop the rushes at the base of my skull. At times my head and neck would shake from the effort of holding back the energy. I didn't always feel in sync with my body. Often my body was in a slightly different position from the one I subjectively experienced.

Around the age of twenty to twenty-two I had a number of trivial psychic experiences. All were witnessed. Several involved dreams predicting certain pieces of mail I received. One involved a very minor auto accident. In a dream of baptism I experienced light-love-joy streaming gently through my body toward the sky. My sexual dreams became more real, and in some I would experience orgasms.

Between my twenty-second and my twenty-fifth year the rushes were not so intense. I could control them at the base of my skull. I experienced shaking and vibrating (visible) which, if intensified, became a rush. Measurable heat usually accompanied the vibrations (99–101 degrees). During this period I spent a year and a half in group therapy. I knew exactly what I needed to do there. The only "resistance" I had was conscious holding back. I had a flow of energy that I was consciously blocking, and now I had a safe and supportive place in which to gradually open the valve. For the first few months I did very little other than allow my body to vibrate, heat up, loosen the clamp on the energy, cry, etc. I understood by now the relationship of the kundalini energy to psychological blocks. (And I appreciate your corroboration in this more than anything.)

During therapy my neck block dissolved undramatically and

was expressed in increased spontaneity. Also during therapy I felt
for the first time the very fine vibrations of the nose and mouth area,
and also the experience of sweetness throughout my entire body. I
had many "special" dreams during this period—of flying, of
illumined landscapes, and of being filled with energy. Some of these
dreams were almost overwhelming, but always they were positive.

From the age of twenty-five to twenty-seven I no longer
experienced fear regarding my kundalini energy experiences. When I
felt the beginnings of shaking and vibrating I would go to where I
could be alone. I sometimes put my body into positions it wanted to
assume. I allowed myself to breathe however my body wanted, often
deep and fast. Sometimes I made sounds. These things were for me
neither voluntary nor involuntary, but "allowed." Sometimes I felt
sexual; sometimes my chest, or my nose and mouth, would vibrate;
sometimes my abdominal muscles would "roll" or contract; som-
times I heard a high-pitched ringing or a low roar in my ears.

I began meditating—in my own style: I would relax and
allow/cause a certain feeling to saturate my body. I realized since
reading your book that the feeling spreads approximately in the
order you mentioned, always beginning with the feet. The feeling is a
sweet porous emptiness and is not just on the surface. The switch
makes my body feel as if it were all one substance/energy. Then
something happens in my eyes. There is a pressure in my eyes
directed to a point behind and between them. Then, sometimes,
something switches there, and I experience a vast dark clearness, and
I am a point in it. Occasionally somewhere along the line my body
feels like it is floating and moving.

During the last couple of years I have been frightened only
once. I felt as if I (my subjective energy-self) were growing bigger
and bigger (around 18 feet), and I was afraid that I would vanish.
The vibrating has occurred only twice that I recall, both times in
"consciousness expanding" situations. I welcome the vibrating and
go along with it, and the result is increased joy—while it lasts—a
kind of grounded ecstasy and openness. I am sure that I could
induce the vibrating by setting up the necessary conditions.

The floating feelings during meditation have increased and are
exactly the same feeling as flying in dreams. One morning in bed,

before waking, I realized that I would have to "move in" a few more inches before I could wake up because I was not quite in sync with my body. So I moved in and promptly woke up. This was not a thought but an experience of my senses. Another new thing that has happened a few times is that I will be asleep but completely conscious (I don't know how else to describe it—I am not talking about lucid dreaming, which I also have), and I can see with my eyes closed. I just lie there in bed and look around the room with my eyes closed and see in incredible detail. This is very unlike dreams. It is exactly like vision.

I recently had a physical sensation dream of "merging"—the word for it was given in the dream. I merged with another person. First the porous, empty, sweet feeling occurred, then our trunks merged, then we had to pull our straying arms into sync.

I am telling you about these dreams because I know that they are the further workings of the kundalini. It is the same energy, becoming more and more refined. And it is the same whether I am waking or sleeping or meditating.

Now, six years after this letter, this woman is no longer meditating. The kundalini activity has quieted down. Her interests lie mainly in the external world. She feels shut down in the navel and heart centers, though she is having frequent psychic experiences, particularly precognition and lucid dreaming.

Chapter 8

SUMMARY OF SIGNS
AND SYMPTOMS

In understanding the physio-kundalini complex, it is useful to distinguish between signs (objective indications) and symptoms (subjective descriptions), and to arrange these into four basic categories—motor, sensory, interpretive, and nonphysiological phenomena.

1. Motor — any manifestation that can be independently observed and measured.

2. Sensory — inner sensations such as lights, sounds, and experiences normally classed as sensations.

3. Interpretive — any mental process that interprets experience.

4. Nonphysiological — phenomena that, taken at face value as genuine occurrences, must involve factors for which physiological explanations are not sufficient.

This fourfold classification is a convenient device. In reality, the physio-kundalini effects—such as automatic body movement, tingling, inner light—are often merely different aspects of a single integrated experience. Another difficulty is that some phenomena belong to two or three categories at once. For instance, objective heat manifestation falls under the motor and sensory categories, whereas "single seeing" is both sensory and interpretive. In this case I have listed the experience under each of the applicable headings for ease of reference, though it is discussed only once.

Motor Phenomena

Automatic Body Movements and Postures. The movements, known in yogic terminology as *kriyas* ("actions"), are spontaneous, although the person may be able to inhibit their occurrence. They can affect any part of the body, including the eyes. Movements may be smooth and sinuous, spasmodic and jerky, or vibratory. They range from muscle twitching to prolonged trembling to the automatic assumption of otherwise difficult and maybe even impossible yogic postures (*asanas, mudras,* etc.). A person may assume these postures without prior knowledge of these yogic practices, which may contain a clue about the way in which they were discovered originally. These automatic movements also include spontaneous crying, laughing, screaming, and whistling.

Unusual Breathing Patterns. According to yogic theory, the life-force (*prana*) pervades the entire body (and the world at large). Prana is closely associated with the breath, which is the mechanism by which the life-force enters, circulates in, and then leaves the body. The yogin, especially the practitioner of Hatha Yoga, aspires to control the flow of the breath/life-force in order to harmonize his bodily energies and increase his vitality. This is thought to prepare the body for the onslaught of the spiritual process, notably the kundalini awakening, which, as we have seen, can have all kinds of undesirable purificatory side effects.

The yogic manipulation of the life-force is technically known as *pranayama,* which is composed of the words *prana* (literally "life") and *ayama* meaning "extension, lengthening." This term is often translated as "breath control," which is adequate enough, providing we remember that the breath is the carrier of the life-force. Some yogins spend many hours a day practicing a variety of pranayama techniques, which typically involve prolonged breath retention.

The automaticities that can occur in the physio-kundalini cycle also include uncommon breathing patterns, such as rapid breathing, shallow breathing, deep breathing, or extended breath retention. As with the other kriyas, these spontaneous alterations of a person's customary breathing pattern can cause a great deal of anxiety. But, according to advanced yogins, these occurrences are a more or less regular feature of the kundalini process. However, some of these authorities warn against the use of pranayama as a means of accelerating the kundalini's ascent.

Paralysis.   During deep meditation the body sometimes becomes temporarily locked into certain postures. The partial paralysis of the two young women whose cases I discussed in Chapter 6 must be considered unusual. Their disabilities developed gradually and remained over longer periods of time, and also interfered with their normal functioning. In both instances, the paralysis subsided when I was able to alleviate their intense fear of the kundalini process through explanation, emotional support, and encouragement. It seems likely that their paralysis was a secondary symptom rather than a primary effect of the physio-kundalini cycle—the change from an underlying organic weakness to a manifest symptom produced by the assault of the kundalini energy.

Sensory Phenomena

Tickling Sensations.   The skin or the inside of the body may tingle, tickle, itch, or vibrate. Apt descriptions are a deep ecstatic tickle and orgasmic feelings. These sensations often start in the feet and legs, or the pelvis, and move up the back to the neck and the crown of the head and then down to the forehead, the face, the throat, and the abdomen, where they terminate. The progression is seldom this ordered, but when it is, we can consider it as a typical physio-kundalini cycle.

Heat and Cold Sensations.   Sensations of temperature extremes, affecting either the whole body or parts of it, occur typically in the kundalini cycle. Like the tingling or tickling sensations, they may also move through the body on occasion, but not always in any recognizable pattern. These sensations of heat and cold may have objective manifestations, which, as we have seen, can include paranormal phenomena.

Inner Lights and Visions.   A variety of photistic (light) experiences may occur during the physio-kundalini process. Some traditions even outline whole sequences of such light phenomena. Swami Muktananda, for instance, distinguished between visions of red light of the size of the whole body, of white and black spots, and of the lentil-sized "blue pearl" in which he saw the matrix of the universe. These or similar lights are sometimes "seen" to illuminate specific areas of the body, such as the spine or the inside of the skull.

Formed visions of varying complexity may also occur, though they are rarer.

I have already spoken of the importance of photistic experiences in the mystical or spiritual traditions of the world. Visions of light were a part of most of the physio-kundalini cases that I was able to study. Psychiatrist Richard Bucke, author of the widely read book *Cosmic Consciousness,* considers this to be the most important criterion for determining whether an experience is "cosmic" or not. He envisions a whole spectrum of light experiences, ranging from subjective symptoms to objective signs. The most subtle experiences are, according to him, those in which illumination is simply a new way of grasping something, as in the "aha!" experience. Then there are visions of internal light or lights. Further along in the spectrum are cases in which the experience of inner light is accompanied by the ability to see a darkened room as illuminated. Still more objective, or externalized, are cases in which *others* perceive an aura or halo of light around the illumined mystic or enlightened being.

Inner Sounds.   Internally perceived sounds include a variety of characteristic noises, such as whistling, hissing, chirping, roaring, and flutelike sounds. These tonal experiences were reported by most of the cases I had occasion to study. They seemed to vary somewhat in accordance with the type of meditation practice. The yogic literature, especially the Sanskrit texts on Hatha Yoga, contain numerous references to this phenomenon, and some even offer a formal arrangement of such sounds, proceeding from the gross to the subtle and ending in the "transcendental" sound called *nada.* This mystical sound is also known as the sacred syllable *om.*

Pain.   "Some of the effects of the Kundalini event are as obvious to the subject as running into a wall. Pain is one of these" (Wolfe 1978, p. 36). Painful sensations are often reported in the head, the eyes, the spine, and other parts of the body. These may begin abruptly, without apparent cause, only to vanish as abruptly and mysteriously after a period of time—from a few seconds to hours and days.

The experience, described in Chapter 6, of the female psychologist who discovered that her headaches were caused by her attempt to control the physio-kundalini process, suggests that pain during the physio-kundalini cycle might be caused by conscious or subconscious resistance to the process. The case of the actress suggests that pain might also occur when the flow of the kundalini force encounters a blockage in the body. This interpretation can explain, for instance, the viselike headaches associated with the kundalini awakening. Itzhak Bentov has addressed this issue in an interview with *New Age* magazine in March 1978. Building on Bentov's speculations, Mineda J. McCleave (1978) has dedicated a whole article, entitled "Kundalini, Headaches and Biofeedback," to this matter. Perhaps it is true to say that of the forty million Americans who are suffering from periodic tension headaches, a good many may be experiencing unpleasant side effects of a partial kundalini arousal. McCleave (1978) made the following observations:

> Tension headaches may be unrecognized symptoms of Kundalini awakening in a nation that has no understanding of the process, but is learning by experience, *what happens*, without knowledge *why* it happens. Migraine may be a precursor to Kundalini activity, or an associated ailment. Cluster headaches, a form of particularly harsh headache that generally strikes males, might be explained by the cyclic nature of Kundalini. These headaches tend to strike most often in the Spring and the Fall, and though many theories are put forth, no one knows with any certainty why they are seasonal. Such headaches may last for half an hour to two hours, approximately, and then disappear for a short while, only to return several times daily, with pain severe enough to cause the victim to pace the floor in agony. They may occur in such clusters for weeks or months, and then completely disappear until the next cluster season . . . It is suspected that

some kind of biorhythmic chemistry may be involved. Kundalini research may help to provide the answer to this mystery. (pp. 23–24)

Interpretive Phenomena

Unusual or Extreme Emotion.   During the physio-kundalini cycle, feelings of ecstasy, bliss, peace, love, devotion, joy, and cosmic harmony may occur almost as readily as feelings of intense fear, anxiety, confusion, depression, and even hatred. In general, especially in the early stages of the process, any of the normal emotions may be experienced with much greater intensity than usual. In the later stages, feelings of bliss, peace, love, and contentment tend to predominate.

Distortions of Thought Processes.   Thinking may be speeded up, slowed down, or altogether inhibited. Thoughts may seem off balance, strange, or irrational. The person may feel on the brink of insanity, enter complete trance states, or may become impulsive and feel alienated and generally confused. Most of the cases I studied involved changes of this type at some stage of the process. Roger Walsh's (1984) personal confession about meditating and thinking is pertinent here. Recalling a ten-day retreat during which he was expected to practice "mindfulness" (the Buddhist vipassana meditation) eighteen hours a day, he wrote:

> The subtlety, complexity, infinite range and number, and entrapping power of the fantasies which the mind creates seem impossible to comprehend, to differentiate from reality while in them, and even more so to describe to one who has not experienced them . . . The power and pervasiveness of these inner dialogues and fantasies left me amazed that we could be so unaware of them during our normal waking life . . . (p. 40)

Walsh further described how he encountered much anxiety, and, once that free-wheeling anxiety had subsided, he felt greatly and unreasonably agitated at the fact that his inexplicable fears had vanished. The kundalini process, like deep meditation, stirs up the sediments of the unconscious and confronts a person with just those psychic materials he or she wishes to inspect least of all. Apart from being unpleasant, this process also holds a certain risk for more unstable individuals.

Detachment. The individual undergoing the physio-kundalini process may feel that he or she is observing, from a distance, his or her own thoughts, feelings, and sensations. This witnessing consciousness differs from mere aloofness or anxious withdrawal inasmuch as the observer-self experiences itself in opposition to the observed mental activities. This condition is hinted at, for instance, in the Sufi expression "the fire of separation" and in the concept of the "seer" (*drashtri*) of the Yoga of Patanjali. This condition does not commonly interfere with the individual's normal functioning.

Dissociation. The state of detachment, or the witnessing consciousness, is attained through the withdrawal of the self from identification or active involvement with its associated mental processes. This detached disposition can be imbalanced when deep psychological resistances, fear, confusion, or social and other environmental pressures are present. In that case, the disposition of detachment may be accompanied by, or result in, hysteria or a state akin to schizophrenia. Also, the person may become egotistically identified with the physio-kundalini process, leading, for instance, to the delusion that he or she has been divinely chosen for some great mission. Imbalances of this kind can usually be overcome in time and through a supportive environment.

Single Seeing. This phenomenon can be easily identified as a distinct state by the typical and graphic metaphors used by those who have had this experience. For example, in his remarkable autobiography, Swami Muktananda (1971) referred to it in the following words:

> My eyes gradually rolled up and became centered on the *akasha* [space] of *sahasrara* [crown center] . . . Now instead of seeing separately, they saw as one. (p. 132)

In a lecture given in February of 1976, he described a state in which his eyes seemed turned equally inward and outward, "seeing" both inner and outer landscapes.

The artist whose case I related in Chapter 6 reported that her "eyes seemed to move separately and the pupils felt like holes which bored into my head and met in the center." Flora Courtois (1970), a modern mystic, wrote of her own experience thus:

> My sight had changed, sharpened to an infinitely small point which moved ceaselessly in paths totally free of the old accustomed ones, as if flowing from a new source . . . It was as if some inner eye, some ancient center of awareness which extended equally and at once in all directions without limit and which had been there all along, had been restored. This inner vision seemed to be focused on infinity in a way that was detached from immediate sight and yet had a profound effect on sight. (pp. 30–35)

This remarkable phenomenon of single seeing is further elucidated by an observation made by C. G. Jung in his 1932 seminar on the kundalini. Asked whether it was not Wotan who lost one eye, he agreed, adding that Osiris did also. Then he went on to say:

> Wotan has to sacrifice his one eye to the well of Mimir, the well of wisdom, which is the unconscious; you see, one eye will remain in the depths or turned towards it. Therefore Jakob Boehme, when he was "enchanted into the centre of nature," as he says, wrote his book about the "Reversed Eye"; one of his eyes was turned inward, it kept on looking into the underworld, which amounts to the loss of one eye; he had no longer two eyes for this world.

Perhaps this is the meaning, or at least part of it, that we must assign to the well-known biblical saying found in Luke 11:34: "The light of the body is the eye; therefore when thine eye is single thy whole body is also full of light." This is the text according to the King James version. In a more recent edition of the Bible the word "single" has been changed to "sound," which is an exoteric reinterpretation of an essentially esoteric experience.

One is also reminded of the single eye of the cyclops in Greek mythology. Here the British classicist E. A. S. Butterworth (1970) has the following insightful comments:

> I know of no possible explanation of the "eye" in the forehead of the Cyclops if it is not the *Ajna-cakra* of a form of yoga. Odysseus, as I suggest, in grinding out the "third eye," shows, in our *Odyssey*, his antagonism to any such view of man. (p. 175)

The "third eye" is iconographically depicted as located in the middle of the forehead. But as Da Love-Ananda (1978a) has made clear, its true location is in the brain core itself.

Alyce Green (1975), interestingly, reported that some of her biofeedback subjects saw an inner vision of a single eye confronting them while they were deeply relaxed. Perhaps we can see in this a symbolic representation of the third eye.

Single seeing has thus many aspects, but in the present context it is understood to be an actual change in visual functioning.

"Great Body" Experience. Occasionally the physio-kundalini process is accompanied by the sensation of being larger than the physical body. Perhaps this phenomenon is an intensified version of the state of joy that is described as "feeling ten feet tall." Here the kinesthetic sense seems to extend beyond the normally experienced boundaries of the body. The person feels as if his or her bodily being has ballooned out.

Nonphysiological Phenomena

Out-of-Body Experiences. Out-of-body experiences (OBEs) involve the subjective feeling of leaving the physical body either as a formless conscious identity or in the form of a supraphysical counterpart ("etheric double" or "astral body," etc.). This phenomenon has come to the attention of the medical establishment through the large number of patients who have reported having had

this experience during anesthesia or while being otherwise unconscious. Medicine treats out-of-body experiences as hallucinations or delusions.

Attempts have been made, however, by parapsychologists to
establish the objective nature of these experiences. There is some
evidence that OBEs can be at least partially objective. This calls in
question the current Western model of the relationship between
brain and consciousness. As in single seeing, the language used to
describe OBEs is so typical that we may think of these experiences as
distinct from other states of divided consciousness.

There are many anecdotal accounts of this experience. An
interesting one is that given by Joyce MacIver (1983). She has had
numerous OBEs, all triggered by her Sufi practice of relaxation and
meditation. Of special interest is her following observation:

> Soon, usually in a matter of five or ten minutes . . . I would
> see the great banks of clouds sweep down and separate, roll back
> and then sweep down again in different formations and colors
> and separate again, always leaving the path at the center . . .
> Simultaneously a feeling of warmth and movement would start
> up from the bottom of my spinal column, rising, growing
> warmer as it moved up, on up toward my shoulder blades,
> accompanied by flashes of heat coming up over my skin—until
> arms, legs, hands and back, and lately abdomen, sometimes felt
> uncomfortably warm. The pusher, as I called this spinal crawler,
> seemed to meet with some block before it could get to my neck.
> No matter. Each time I did the exercise it seemed to strike out
> harder and harder and, lately, toward the end of the sixth week, I
> noticed flashes of light, seemingly in the room and near my body,
> beyond the Private Theatre, appearing in my closed eyelids.
> (pp. 87–88)

As I wrote in an appendix to Joyce MacIver's book, "It is very
clear to me that her journeys into the hidden levels of reality had a
positive, healing and revelatory effect on her life . . . This conclusion
is frequently countered with the argument that such experiences are
only possible if you believe in them. To this argument I answer, yes,
such experiences are only possible if you believe in them and may in
fact be created by that belief. This answer does not diminish the

value of the experience, instead it leaves open and unrestricted our definition of human potential and provides unrestricted horizons for the depth and scope of spiritual growth" (pp. 129–130).

For further data on the OBE phenomenon the works by Robert Monroe (1972), Sylvan J. Muldoon (1968, 1969), and Robert Crookall (1970) can be recommended.

Psychic Perceptions.   Psychic abilities and experiences, notably the ability to obtain information through means other than the known physical senses, are frequently reported by people in whom the kundalini process is active. Such paranormal experiences, if confirmed, would have to be listed under the "sensory" category and, like OBEs, would require explanations that go beyond today's neurophysiological models.

In some cases, these psychic perceptions are clearly the result of an awakened kundalini. Often, however, they precede the awakening. This may indicate that the physio-kundalini cycle is more readily triggered in people who are naturally more sensitive and psychic.

Correlations with Bentov's Model

Motor Signs and Symptoms.   The cerebral current may stimulate the motor cortex or thalamic centers associated with group muscle movements, such as the posturing reflexes. The apparent non-specificity of some of these movements may indicate that the focus of disturbance is deep in the brain, rather than in the cortex. Breathing patterns may be similarly stimulated and paralysis is probably a secondary effect, as already noted.

Body Sensations.   These may be attributed to direct stimulation of the sensory cortex by the current generated in the cerebral hemispheres. The characteristic sequence of affected body parts corresponds to their sequence of representation in the sensory cortex: first the toes, then the limbs, back, head, eyes, and face, to the throat, and finally the abdominal area represented just above the temporal lobe. According to Bentov's model the earliest body sensations in the kundalini process appear in the foot, especially in the left big toe represented in the brain's central sulcus. (The holy river Ganges is said to have originated from the large toe of God. In Siddha Yoga the teacher's feet are special objects of veneration, particularly the large toe.) The exact correspondence between the sequence of stimulation in the typical physio-kundalini cycle and the sequence of representation in the sensory cortex gives strong support to at least this aspect of Bentov's model.

It is interesting to note that in this model the throat and abdomen are the last sites to open, indicating the completion of the cycle. The importance of the throat is traditionally recognized in one of the esoteric names given to the kundalini, namely Vag-Ishvari, or "Goddess of Speech." Supposedly, it is after the throat opening that the legendary magical powers of an adept are greatly magnified.

Heat and Cold Sensations. These may be caused by hypothalamic stimulation. The representation of the body in this area of the brain is less specific than it is in the cortex, which may explain the lack of regularity in the movement of these particular sensations. Objective manifestations of extreme heat are difficult to explain with Bentov's model alone. It does not contradict them but suggests that other factors are also involved in the kundalini phenomenon.

Light and Sound Phenomena. These could be due to stimulation near the lateral and medial geniculate regions, as well as to standing waves generated in the ventricles. The usual lack of formed elements could be due to the large distance of the circuit from cortical representation for light and sound. Formed visions and voices may indicate a spreading of the stimulation to adjacent associative areas for speech, sound, and vision. If they were psychically determined, they would have quite a different and unknown origin. Certainly objective manifestations of light, if confirmed, would also require explanations beyond our present knowledge.

Pain. Pain might occur when the current generated in the brain meets with some resistance that is not easily overcome. The perception of the pain may be referred out and may seem to come from various parts of the body, or motor stimulation could cause tension generating pain in the periphery itself. In practice, it makes little difference whether these impurities, or blocks to the rise of the kundalini current, are actually located in the cakras of the spinal axis, as the yogins claim, or in peripheral body parts, or in specific brain regions, or at some more subtle level of the mind. These different possibilities are not mutually exclusive, and the net result is the same.

Emotions and Distorted Thought Processes.   These are not inconsistent with Bentov's model but are too complex to be explained by it at this time.

Detachment and Dissociation.   Wilder Penfield (1958) reported experiences akin to detachment and dissociation upon direct stimulation of area 39 of the cortex. Thus they could be a simple result of the circulating current, or they could have a more subtle psychological origin.

Single Seeing and the Great Body.   These experiences are not inconsistent with Bentov's model but cannot be explained by it thus far.

Out-of-Body and Psychic Experiences.   Bentov's model does not offer an explanation for these phenomena, which have been objectively confirmed, though it does give guidelines for the direction in which research might profitably move. I will say more about this at the end of the next chapter.

Kundalini: Classical and Clinical

As I have already explained, there are two major models of kundalini activity. On the one hand, there is the classical model formulated in the Yoga and Tantra scriptures of India. On the other hand, there is Bentov's physiological model, together with the kind of clinical observations presented in this book.

Those aspects of the process that could have a purely physiological basis I have designated as *physio-kundalini*, and the majority of my clinical observations fall within this category. These physio-kundalini signs and symptoms differ in important respects from the descriptions found in the yogic literature. The most notable difference concerns the pathway taken by the kundalini energy in its ascent and the bodily sensations associated with this.

According to the classical model, the kundalini awakens, or is awakened, at the base of the spine, travels straight up the central axis of the body, and completes its journey when it reaches the crown of the head. Along this route, there are said to be several centers of psychic energy. These centers, or cakras, contain impurities that must be removed before the kundalini energy can continue in its upward course.

By contrast, the clinical picture is that the kundalini energy travels up the legs and the back to the top of the head, then down the face, through the throat, to a terminal point in the abdominal area. What is the relationship between these two descriptions?

First of all, we must appreciate that the yogic accounts, in addition to being dogmatic, are often very subtle. Western scientists argue that the actual location of sensory perception is in the sensory cortex, even though the sensations are felt to be in the periphery. Similarly, the yogins might mean that the sensations, blocks, and openings (such as the throat opening), which are felt to occur in various body parts, are in some subtle way represented in the spinal cakras.

Still another possibility is suggested by the experience of one of Swami Muktananda's students who told me (in 1975) that he felt the kundalini energy spreading throughout his body, but especially descending from his forehead over his face to his throat, then to his chest and abdomen, then to the base of the spine, and only then into and up the center of the spine itself. He further remarked that the sensation in the spine is more subtle and difficult to perceive than that of the peripheral areas. A possible reason for this, he suggested, is that perhaps in his case the energy had not yet entered significantly into the spinal axis.

Another point of difference between the classical and the

clinical descriptions is the time factor. All the characteristic features of the physio-kundalini complex are included in the classical descriptions. And yet we find quite "ordinary" people who complete the physio-kundalini cycle in a matter of months, whereas the yogic scriptures assign a much longer period—generally several years—to the complete kundalini process in the case of the most advanced initiates. Here we have the suggestion that the full kundalini awakening is a more comprehensive process of which the physio-kundalini cycle is only a part. It is quite feasible that the physio-kundalini is a separate mechanism that may be activated as part of a complete kundalini awakening. It is too early to draw any final conclusions.

Much of the problem stems from the difficulty of comparing different stages, whereas in fact many of the processes occur concurrently. Individual differences further complicate the picture. However, it is possible to bring some clarity into this matter by regarding the kundalini awakening as a purificatory process. If the impurities, or imbalances, have any objective reality, it should be possible to demonstrate their existence by physiological and psychological tests, and to correlate their removal with specific signs and symptoms observed clinically. Since Bentov's model explains how this process may be triggered and since we know how it may be recognized in its initial stages, long-term case studies covering the entire course of the kundalini unfolding are a logical next step in these investigations. They would be invaluable in documenting specific objective ways in which the kundalini process is beneficial.

Bentov's model can account, in detail, for many of the signs and symptoms observed in the course of a kundalini awakening. Even if it ultimately proves to be only partially correct, or to explain only a part of the total kundalini phenomenon, it is of enormous heuristic value at this point.

What distinguishes Bentov's model from all previous attempts to explain the kundalini is that it generates further hypotheses and even suggests a number of experiments to test them. Here are some ideas:

1. Measure the very weak magnetic fields around the head of an

expert meditator, following methods such as those described by Brenner, Williamson, and Kaufman (1975).

2. Determine at what stage of meditation the irregular microtremor changes to a resonant vibration.

3. Develop a biofeedback system to aid meditators in reaching resonance.

4. Study the effects of magnetic stimulation on one side and then on both sides of the head.

5. Study light, heat, and sound sensations reported by meditators and determine which of these can be correlated with physically measurable conditions.

Chapter 9

THE KUNDALINI CYCLE: DIAGNOSIS AND THERAPY

Diagnostic Considerations

The clinical data at hand indicates a clear distinction between the physio-kundalini complex and psychosis. These findings also furnish a number of criteria for distinguishing between these two conditions. In some of the cases presented in this book, we have seen that a schizophrenia-like condition can result when the person undergoing the kundalini experience receives negative feedback either through social pressure or through the resistances created by earlier conditioning.

Evidence that these conditions are distinct and separate is supplied particularly by two of my cases. The first is the case of the female artist, which I outlined in Chapter 6. The other case is not included in this book. It involved a person who became "psychotic" after being confined to a mental institution for inappropriate behavior. Each of them reported that during their stay in their respective mental institutions they were quite sure that they (and several of the other patients) could tell who among them were "crazy" and who were just "far-out and turned on."

Possibly this is a situation where "it takes one to know one," and a person whose own kundalini is active can intuitively sense the kundalini state of another. This is of special interest, as such people could be consulted when assistance is needed to decide which way the balance lies between the two processes in any particular case (see Appendix 2 on the Masts of India).

Clinicians usually have a finely tuned sense of what is psychotic. For the most part, it is this sense for the "smell" of psychosis that tells us if a patient is unbalanced or whether he or she is instead inundated with more positive psychic forces. Also, trained clinicians generally have a feeling for whether a patient is dangerous to himself or herself and to others. Individuals who experience hostility or anger in the early phases of kundalini awakening are in my experience rarely inclined to dramatize their violent emotions.

Furthermore, those in whom the kundalini elements predominate are usually much more objective about themselves and have an interest in sharing their experiences and troubles. Those on the psychotic side tend to be very oblique, secretive, and totally preoccupied with ruminations about some vague but apparently significant subjective aspect of their experience that they can never quite communicate.

My clinical data together with Bentov's model allows me to highlight several more distinguishing features. Sensations of heat are common in kundalini states but are rare in psychosis. Also very typical are feelings of vibration or fluttering, tingling, and itching that move in definite patterns over the body, usually in the sequence described earlier. But these patterns may be irregular in atypical cases or in those who have preconceived ideas of how the kundalini energies should circulate. In addition to this, bright lights may be seen internally. There may be pain, especially in the head, which arises suddenly and ceases equally suddenly during critical phases in the process. Unusual breathing patterns are common, as well as other spontaneous movements of the body. Noises such as chirping and whistling sounds are heard, but seldom do voices intrude in a negative way, as is the case in psychotic states. When voices are heard, they are perceived to come from within and are not mistaken for outer realities.

My clinical findings support the view that the kundalini force is positive and creative. Each of my kundalini clients is now successful in his or her own terms. They all report that they can handle stress more easily and have become more relational. The classical cases indicate that special capacities (known as *siddhis* or "powers"), as well as deep inner peace, may result from the completion of the kundalini process. But in the initial stages, stress induced by the experience itself, coupled with a negative attitude from oneself or others, may be overwhelming and cause severe imbalance.

Experience suggests that such cases are best approached with understanding, strength, and gentle support. Earlier I described the case of the writer whose spontaneous trances had disturbed him greatly. They ceased altogether when I encouraged him to enter a trance state voluntarily. By making a distinction between psychotic and psychically active, I had communicated to him the attitude that his trances were valid and meaningful. Because of my own acceptance of his experience, he was also able to accept it. The trances ceased to control him as soon as he gave up his resistance to them and their underlying forces.

Similarly, the female psychologist suffered from severe headaches, which stopped as soon as she ceased trying to control the process, accepting it instead. The pain, in other words, did not result from the kundalini process itself but from the person's resistance to it. I suspect this is true of all the negative effects of the physio-kundalini mechanism.

Symptoms caused by the physio-kundalini will disappear spontaneously over time. Because we are dealing essentially with a purificatory or balancing process, and since each person represents a finite system, the process is self-limiting. Disturbances must also not be viewed as pathological. They are, rather, therapeutic inasmuch as they lead to a removal of potentially pathological elements.

The kundalini force arises spontaneously from deep within the body-mind, and is apparently self-directing. Tension and imbalance thus result not from the process itself but from conscious or subconscious interference with it. Helping a person to understand and accept what is happening to him or her may be the best we can do. Usually the process, when left alone, will find its own natural pace and balance. However, if it has already become too rapid or violent, my experience suggests that its course can be moderated by introducing a heavier diet and vigorous exercise and by suspending meditation.

Those in whom the physio-kundalini process is most readily activated and in whom it is most likely to become violent and disturbing are those with especially sensitive nervous systems—the natural psychics. Many of my cases had had some kind of psychic experience prior to their kundalini awakening. Natural psychics tend to find the physio-kundalini experience so intense that they will not engage in the regular classical meditation methods that commonly enhance the kundalini process. Sometimes, if they do not wish to refrain from meditating altogether, they may adopt some mild form of their own choosing. Much of their anxiety may be due to misunderstanding and ignorance of the physio-kundalini process. Rather than increasing their fear, one should obviously give them the knowledge and confidence to allow the process to progress at the maximum comfortable, natural rate.

Clearly, much could be accomplished by changing attitudes, first in those experiencing the kundalini phenomenon, but ultimately in our society as a whole. This would benefit all of us who need viable models in our spiritual quest. Unfortunately, in our Western civilization, spiritual values and attitudes are generally suppressed. Some other cultures are more advanced in this regard, and they recognize the positive contribution made by spiritually or psychically developed individuals. Thus, in Bali the trance state serves an important adaptive function for the children. As Richard Katz (1973) has shown, the African Bushmen use trance as a central ritual that promotes social cohesion. I was informed by J. Scutch (1974) that in South Africa a psychic condition, which Western psychiatry would probably identify as an acute schizophrenic break, is a prerequisite for initiation into the priesthood of one tribe. In the Himalayan countries, trance mediums fulfill an important social function. Many more examples could readily be given.

By contrast, how many creative people in our culture are suffering because of diagnostic mistakes? I feel that the healing profession has a special obligation to make every effort to correct these mistakes. Recognition of the kundalini phenomenon as a nonpsychotic process is a part of this. It is tragic that potentially charismatic folks like shamans, trance mediums, and God-intoxicated individuals (similar to the Masts of India) might actually find themselves in custodial care in our society. Possibly there are many now who, despite their eccentricities, should be released so that they can enrich our lives.

The problem is to identify them among the other inmates of our mental institutions. Here Meher Baba's work with the Masts, as mentioned in Appendix 2, might serve as a useful precedent (see Donking 1948). If it is true, as I have already suggested, that "it takes one to know one," such people could indeed be invaluable in our diagnosis and therapeutic support of kundalini cases.

Of those undergoing the kundalini process without preparation, not a few tend to feel quite insane, at least at times. By behaving normally and keeping silent about their experience, they may avoid being labeled schizophrenic, or being hospitalized, or sedated. But imagine their sense of isolation and the suffering caused by their separation from others. We must reach these people, their families, and the larger culture with the information necessary to help them recognize their condition as a blessing, not a curse. Certainly, we must no longer subject people in the midst of this rebirth process to drugs or shock therapy—approaches which are poles apart from creative self-development and spiritual maturation. Instead, we must begin to acknowledge that these individuals, though they may be confused and fearful, are already undergoing therapy from within—a therapy that is far superior to any that modern medicine could administer from without.

Kundalini as Therapy

Several of my kundalini cases are especially interesting because they serve as support for my contention that the kundalini process can be looked upon as being inherently therapeutic. A psychologist-writer was hospitalized for three months thirty years ago. He had been diagnosed as suffering from a psychotic break, characterized by disturbances in judgment, flight of ideas, grandiosity, and over-activity. After that episode he was somewhat unstable, suffering from a chronic mild depression. Nevertheless, he made his living as a therapist, occasionally being very effective, but constantly becoming involved in countertransference problems (that is, over-involvement with his clients). At other times, he was unable to provide for himself adequately.

In 1974 he became a disciple of Swami Muktananda, a master of Siddha Yoga. He found that his stay at the Swami's Indian hermitage and the contact with that adept and with other spiritual practitioners proved a very potent therapy. Signs of kundalini awakening began to appear early in his involvement with Swami Muktananda, and it led to, or at least was accompanied by, a prodigious increase in productivity in his writing. He also began to enjoy new depths in his interpersonal relationships and gained a surer grasp on his life. I saw him frequently both before and during this important period in his life and can attest to the dramatic strengthening of his whole personality structure, character, and his ways of dealing with the world, both inner and outer.

Another case, a female psychologist, now in her mid-fifties, had been severely depressed for many years and had even made two serious suicide attempts by overdosing on sleeping pills. She remained in a coma for several days following each episode. Her only extended hospitalization occurred prior to these suicide attempts, as a result of her depression following the birth of her first child. For years she held a responsible position as an administrator, and she was also a successful psychotherapist. During this time she herself was undergoing psychotherapy, including a classical psychoanalysis.

In 1972 this woman attended a meditation retreat during which she spent many hours each day in meditation. Within a short time she began to have spontaneous kundalini experiences. Subsequently she became a student of Swami Muktananda. I got to know her in 1973. During the first year of our acquaintance she was somewhat withdrawn and reserved. But later she blossomed into a secure, intact, fun-loving person. She tells me that she has not known a day of depression since. My observations confirm her self-appraisal.

I recall four psychics, each of whom had been diagnosed as suffering from some sort of convulsive disorder. In each case there was a marked relief in symptoms and in their need for anti-convulsive medication after finding and using their psychic talents.

Some other creative pursuit might have proven equally liberating. These four people chose to become professional psychics, and although no claim is made, based on this evidence, for a causal relationship between their new energy investment and the ameliora- tion of their symptoms, it is suggestive. I feel quite certain that at a higher level of functioning, such as may become effective through the kundalini process, there will accrue all kinds of benefits, including better health and emotional balance.

Of course, as we have seen, the kundalini process can also be disruptive. If left alone, a person may well suffer doubts and fears that could easily be handled in a supportive environment like a spiritual hermitage or monastery, where the disturbing side effects of a kundalini awakening are rightly understood, accepted, and to some extent even welcomed.

Without such a setting, however, those who experience this force may react in a number of undesirable ways. Naive individuals may interpret the experience as an inner change so profound and upsetting as to be a convincing indication of loss of sanity. This is essentially what happened in the case of the female artist and that of the actress described in Chapter 6. Also in at least one instance (that of the middle-aged housewife) the confusion and turmoil arising from a spontaneous kundalini awakening led to psychic inflation and delusions of grandeur.

The female psychologist handled her inner disruption by becoming a member of various groups, and by finding supportive teachers and therapists. It was necessary for her to make use of these aids for a year or more before she could continue on her own. The scientist, whose understanding was even more adequate and whose situation was quite supportive, was able to function by simply cutting down on the intensity of his meditations.

It should be clear by now that physicians are well advised to be alert for the symptom patterns of an active kundalini when making a diagnosis. Neurologists with diagnostic problems mimicking patho- logical conditions may gain valuable diagnostic clues by reviewing the patient's meditation history. In this way they may delay or completely avoid harsh and inappropriate diagnostic procedures. Psychotherapists dealing with hysterical overlays or psychotic reac- tions to kundalini awakening are reminded that beneath the neurosis, or psychosis, a process is occurring that is far beyond our ordinary understanding of psychopathology and of the kind of ecstatic states described, for instance, by William James (1929).

In addition to psychotherapy, if indicated, I recommend that persons suspected of kundalini problems be urged to consult someone with experience in this area. Of course, selecting a helping person may be most difficult. Unless the physician is experienced and has explored the available resources, he or she may be unable to do more than recommend that the patient seek out such an individual. In some cases it may be appropriate to refer the patient to a spiritual teacher who is known to be familiar with the kundalini phenomenon and may even, as was the case with the late Swami Muktananda, be able to induce it by way of psychic transmission.

I must, however, sound a word of caution here. I firmly believe that methods designed specifically to hasten kundalini arousal, such as the breath control exercises known as *pranayama*, are hazardous, unless practiced directly under the guidance of a competent spiritual teacher, or guru, who should have gone through the whole kundalini process himself or herself. Deliberate practice of yogic breathing techniques may prematurely unleash titanic inner forces for which the unprepared individual has no means of channeling and control. The kundalini can be forced, but only to one's own detriment.

Epilogue

In scientific circles it is something of a truism that many experiments with surprising and unexplained outcomes remain unpublished, whereas those that support favorite hypotheses get into print. In other words, the business of science is not as objective as scientific ideology would have it. This explains why the more esteemed scientific journals, which of course are also the most conservative, have given very little space to the kind of unusual phenomena that are mentioned in this book. However, there are many stalwart researchers who are not discouraged by this but who continue to dedicate their lives to exploring psychospiritual realities.

One of these maverick scientists is Hiroshi Motoyama. He has done much to verify the cakra system and also the acupuncture meridians through his sophisticated electromagnetic equipment. It was at his laboratory in Tokyo, Japan, that Itzhak Bentov and I did a series of experiments that showed amplitude differences in the body's micromotions on the right and left sides of the head. The motion on the left was fifty percent greater. Shortly after we had noted this remarkable difference, we chanced upon another significant discovery: When our subject went into a deep meditative state, this right-left difference was almost equalized.

In ordinary consciousness, the EEG amplitude at one side of the brain is greater than at the other. With feedback and patience a person can balance this difference, and at that point he or she feels profound peace and tranquillity. Perhaps our finding is a physical counterpart of this psychological state.

J. Millay (1976) observed that subjective reports of peacefulness, centeredness, and light were common among a group of students who achieved 7- to 13-Hz EEG phase coherence between the right and the left cerebral hemisphere. Another confirmation of the link between mental states and physiology is seen in the work of Manfred Clynes (see Jonas 1972). He has shown that an emotion can be recorded by a simple transducer sensitive to lateral and vertical pressure. Clynes had his subjects fantasize a particular emotion and press on the transducer simultaneously. This created a characteristic signature or waveform for each emotion.

Sylvia Brody and Saul Axelrod (1970) noted that fetal responses studied by them had pattern, direction, and effect. Later, William Condon and Louis Sander found that the apparent random movements of infants were synchronized with adult speech they heard. Summarizing the work of these two scientists, Joseph Chilton Pearce (1980) stated that as adults we have our own personal repertoire of micromuscular movements coordinating with our use of and reception to speech. These studies, similar to those I mentioned earlier, are further evidence for a sensory-motor link.

My colleagues and I, as well as others, have attempted to measure physiological correlates of meditators' reported sensations of heat, light, and sound. As noted in the case histories of meditators undergoing the kundalini awakening, we did observe temperature changes in one case. Such changes could be made visible on recently developed medical thermographic equipment, without the need for attaching temperature transducers to the bodies of meditating subjects. Other investigators, particularly R. Dobrin (1975), have described the use of sensitive photomultiplier tubes to detect low-intensity ultraviolet light from the bodies of experimental subjects, but so far little attention has been paid to correlating such measurements with meditative processes. Our attempts to measure physiological correlates of meditators' sound sensations were unsuccessful. Further work along all of these lines, using improved equipment and experimental procedures, is called for. It will help demonstrate the extent to which there is an objective basis for the subjective reports of meditators.

We did an interesting experiment—which has not, to my knowledge, been confirmed or replicated—using Hiroshi Moto-yama's electric field sensor, or "cakra measuring device." When the subject sat quietly in this machine, we could observe the usual EEG waveform. After a few minutes of deep meditation, probably at the point where the subject felt he or she had transcended the ordinary consciousness, there suddenly appeared a diminution of these signals and a corresponding increase in amplitude in a higher frequency band, one which our experimenters had not been equipped to detect. To our surprise, this new waveform was in the frequency range of 350 to 500 Hz, much higher than the 0- to 50-Hz frequency range of a normal EEG waveform. These higher frequency EEG signals could be an easily measured physiological indicator of certain meditative states and out-of-body experiences, or of biloca-tion of consciousness. If so, a subject full of mystery and fascination for centuries can now become a new frontier for science.

Chapter 10

THE KUNDALINI AND
SPIRITUAL LIFE

Kundalini awakenings can and do happen, as I have shown, even without any spiritual preparation or meditation practice. This raises the question of the role of the kundalini in the spiritual process. According to some schools of thought, spiritual life is dependent on the kundalini power. These schools insist that the latent energy of the body-mind must be galvanized into activity and raised along the bodily axis to the crown of the head before a real spiritual transformation can occur.

If this were true, however, we would have to discount many spiritual traditions. There have been and still are genuine mystics who have never consciously experienced the psychophysical symptoms associated with the kundalini arousal. They may know nothing of headaches, burning sensations, painful currents of energy shooting from the feet or the base of the spine up into the head, or of the seven or more wheels of energy in the body. And yet they may experience the unitive consciousness, tranquillity, and bliss. They may even be psychic.

If we assume, with Gopi Krishna (1971), that the kundalini is a fundamental evolutionary mechanism underlying all psychic and spiritual phenomena, then there are two explanations for the absence of physio-kundalini symptoms in many spiritual practitioners and accomplished mystics. The first explanation is that these individuals are relatively free of the kind of obstructions or psychophysical resistances that tend to complicate the kundalini process in others. The second is that their psychospiritual realizations are the result of only a partial awakening of the kundalini power. Both explanations have their supporters, and my personal opinion is that without additional research the matter cannot be conclusively settled. What we can consider further, however, is the relationship between the kundalini and authentic spirituality. Granted that the kundalini fulfills an evolutionary function in the body-mind, does this mechanism really have anything to do with the spiritual process? It depends on what we mean by "spiritual." Here we must note that spirituality is generally understood to consist in attitudes and techniques leading to psychic experiences or powers and extraordinary "enlarged" states of consciousness.

This would clearly make spirituality a matter of the evolving nervous system. Some people indeed make this claim. A different, more radical point of view is put forward by the adept Da Love-Ananda (Da Free John). His point of view is perfectly consistent with the great nondualist traditions of the world, such as Advaita Vedanta and Mahayana Buddhism. His argument is, very simply, that most so-called spiritual accomplishments are *experiences* generated within the body-mind and are therefore not truly self-transcending. They are products of the great search for fulfillment or happiness.

Authentic spirituality, by contrast, is founded in the moment-to-moment transcendence of the ego, the body-mind, and all possible experiential states. It has nothing to do with the search for God or higher evolutionary possibilities. It requires living on the basis of the intuitive recognition that there is no real separation from Life, or God, or the Transcendental Reality. Da Love-Ananda (1980) put it thus:

> Our obligation is not to invert and go elsewhere to God, nor to extrovert and exploit ourselves in the self-possessed or anti-ecstatic mood that presumes God to be absent or nonexistent. Our obligation is to Awaken beyond our selves, beyond the phenomena of body and mind into That in which body and mind inhere. (p. 18)

Such awakening, or self-transcendence, is possible only when we begin to understand that the egoic body-mind is by tendency recoiling from everything or, as Da Love-Ananda would say, is always "avoiding relationship." In his own words:

> You have been contracted upon yourself with emotional force, and no amount of thinking, considering, experiencing, desiring, exploiting, and manipulating yourself in the world can affect that contraction. No awakening of the kundalini touches it. It has nothing to do with the kundalini. You can have kundalini experiences until you are yawning with boredom, yet you will not have touched this emotional recoil at all. (p. 20)

Spiritual practice is primarily a matter of dealing with this automatic gesture of emotional withdrawal from the larger life or, if you will, God. It is this continuous gesture that is the ego, and it is the ego habit that prevents God-realization, or enlightenment, in the moment. Therefore, spiritual practice consists in constantly going beyond the wall of the ego, in reaching out and embracing all life fearlessly, with an open heart. There must be complete clarity and integrity in one's feelings. Most people are "collapsed at the heart." They are in doubt of God, others, and themselves. Their feeling being is stunted.

In their unhappiness, they search endlessly for ways to feel better. If they cannot console themselves with the usual pleasures of sex, food, or power, they look for other means by which to stimulate their nervous systems. They become "spiritual" seekers, exploring the potential of their own bodies and minds. And yet, their escape from the basic feeling of dissociation and contraction is destined to be futile. One cannot transcend what one does not recognize and understand.

No amount of mystical fireworks in the synapses of the brain can help overcome the crunch at the heart. Once the vision or experience of bliss is over, the person simply returns to his or her state of emotional distress. Then he or she will have to make renewed efforts to stimulate the nervous system or force the kundalini into higher centers in order to feel blissful again. In this respect, psychic or mystical experiences are little different from orgasms. Whether a person stimulates the sexual organs or the brain, the result is always only a psychophysical experience, not

God-realization. In an unpublished talk dated July 8, 1978, Da Love-Ananda remarked:

> The lust for the kundalini in the brain core is exactly the same as the lust for the kundalini in the sex center. It is using that mechanism in a different direction. But neither direction is toward God . . . Attachment to the brain through the inversion of attention in the kundalini, or the Life-Current, is traditionally promoted as the way to God. This is an error that has crept into the spiritual traditions. The way to God is not via the kundalini. The awakening of the kundalini and becoming absorbed in the brain core is not God-realization. It has nothing to do with God-realization. It is simply a way of tuning into an extraordinary evolutionary mechanism. The way to God-realization is the one by which that mechanism is understood and transcended completely.

Authentic spirituality is thus down to earth. It begins and continues by taking responsibility for one's emotional recoil—one's loveless-ness, distrust, mood of betrayal, sense of conflict, and fear. This is what Da Love-Ananda (1980) means by the Way of the Heart.

> The heart is the key to the practice of real or spiritual life. People tend to focus on the dimensions of the mind or the body, and to lose the focus of the heart. Nevertheless, the principle of spirituality is at the heart, and the fire of the spiritual process is awakened there. That fire is not situated at the perineum, nor is it up at the crown. It is at the heart, at the place of Infinity, the root of the being, the feeling core of the body-mind. (p. 27)

When speaking of the fire of the spiritual process, Da Love-Ananda is, of course, not pointing to any heat sensations, which belong to the realm of the physio-kundalini. He uses the word metaphorically. The spiritual fire is the subjective sense of catharsis, of being gradually purified of all presumptions, opinions, illusions, and delusions as well as all attachments and preferences—that is to say, every single movement within our own consciousness by which we deny or hide from Reality. This purification, which is accomplished by staying in place rather than by going on any quest, whether internal or external, can be accompanied by all kinds of mental and physical symptoms—from discomfort to sickness, including fevers and manifestations of heat in different parts of the body.

Da Love-Ananda speaks from his own experience. He is thoroughly familiar with a wide range of kundalini symptoms, and knows and insists on the difference between kundalini states, mystical experiences, psychic phenomena, and the great spiritual awakening, which has nothing to do with the nervous system. He knows the difference between the kundalini power and the transcendental Power (or Shakti), which is the infinite and limitless dynamic aspect of the Ultimate Reality itself.

Availing himself of Hindu metaphysics, he speaks of that Ultimate Reality as Shiva-Shakti. Shiva represents the Consciousness aspect, whereas Shakti represents the Power aspect. But the two are only distinguishable on the conceptual level. In truth, they are the same single Intensity. Da Love-Ananda (1978b) remarked:

> All that arises is already the union of *Siva* and *Shakti*. It is not necessary to raise the *kundalini* one inch. It is already raised. It is continually rising. And it is continually descending. It is a circle of conductivity about the Sun, the Heart [or the essential Self]. When manifest existence is lived from the point of view of the Heart, all ascent and all descent is already and continually accomplished. (p. 85)

From this perspective, the kundalini energy is simply a manifestation of that same single Intensity, or Reality. It is a phenomenon of the evolving human body-mind before it is fully awakened.

The enlightened teacher communicates Shiva-Shakti, or Consciousness-Power, by his or her mere existence. He or she is in fact not different from that Reality because he or she no longer suffers from the presumption of being a finite being with a body and mind that is ultimately separate from other beings. An enlightened person lives as, and out of, the fullness of the single Reality. Therefore his or her sheer presence has transformative power, which is of advantage to those who can attune themselves to it. As Da Love-Ananda (1978b) explained:

> The *Shakti* of the true *Guru* is not simply or exclusively the *kundalini shakti*, which is always returning to Truth, seeking the

> Truth, seeking the union that is Truth. The *Shakti* that flows
> through the true *Guru* is already the Truth. It is the Force of
> Truth. (p. 116)

The teacher's communication of that which is Real has a
purifying effect on the disciple who receives this spiritual transmission. And that is its whole purpose. The teacher's transmission
can have very different effects in the disciple. It can lead to utterly
blissful states or violent emotional reactivity, feelings of well-being
or episodes of illness. Regardless of the effects, the primary function
of spiritual transmission is to intensify the disciple's whole life. For
it is through such intensification that he or she becomes sensitive to,
and intelligent about, the gesture of recoil or self-contraction. Only
then can there be real change or transformation. And one indication
of real change is the willingness to transcend even the most blissful
experience, until there is the firm realization that there is only the
one unqualified Reality.

That all this is not mere philosophy is clear from Da Love-
Ananda's numerous writings and the accounts of his disciples. He
speaks with authority from personal realization. In his spiritual
autobiography, *The Knee of Listening,* he describes how, until his
second or third year, his sense of identity was that of being a bubble
of energy, light, and flawless joy, which he calls the "bright." Upon
the loss of this extraordinary condition, he set out on a quest that
was to last until 1970.

As a child he would periodically pass into what appeared to be
feverish deliriums during which he reawakened to the condition of
the "bright." Although the "bright" had receded, it was still
effective in him as a mysterious impulse. It was, however, only
during his years at Columbia University that he began to systemati-
cally explore the possibilities of the human body-mind, ever in
search of the "bright." One night, feeling he had exhausted his
search, he had the following experience:

> Then, quite suddenly, in a moment, I experienced a total
> revolution of energy and awareness in myself. An absolute sense
> of understanding opened and arose at the extreme end of all this
> consciousness. And all of the energy of thought that moved
> down into that depth appeared to reverse its direction at some

unfathomable point. The rising impulse caused me to stand, and I felt a surge of force draw up out of my depths and expand, filling my whole body and every level of my consciousness with wave on wave of the most beautiful and joyous energy . . . My head had begun to ache with the intense energy that saturated my brain . . . And at last I wore myself out wandering in the streets, so that I returned to my room. (1978c, p. 14)

By the time he arrived at Stanford University, in 1961, he had become certain that the enlightened state was prevented by a simple mechanism in his own consciousness. He now set out to rigorously observe its activity. He borrowed the Greek mythological figure of Narcissus to symbolize that mechanism of loveless self-encapsulation, the ego habit. He had many remarkable psychic and mystical experiences during that time. One experience is of particular interest here. During a formal LSD session at the Veterans Administration Hospital, in Mountain View, California, he was overwhelmed by a profound emotion, beginning at the base of the spine and traveling up to the heart, the throat, the back of the head, and culminating at the crown of the head. He wrote about this experience as follows:

> I had become conscious of the formal structure of our living being, analogous to the nervous system, but, even more than that, what is called in Indian and occult literature the "chakra body" or the awakened "Kundalini Shakti" . . . It was this very "form," this ordinary and spiritual body, which I knew as a child and recognized as the "bright." (1978c, pp. 18–19)

He also would frequently experience the "spherical form" of the so-called astral body, as well as a sensation of "thumbs" pressing in on him. Although these experiences held a certain fascination for him, his primary motivation was to understand the mechanism of the "self-contraction." He then realized that he was in need of a teacher.

In 1964 he entered a discipleship under Albert Rudolph, known as "Rudi" or Swami Rudrananda. This former student of Swami Muktananda taught a type of Kundalini Yoga that was based on self-effort rather than self-transcendence and grace. With Rudi, Da Love-Ananda had his first experiences of the transmission of psychic energy from teacher to disciple.

Finding that Rudi's Yoga contradicted his own intuition that the spiritual process is founded in self-surrender rather than any effortful self-discipline, Da Love-Ananda turned to Swami Muktananda for help. After only three days at the Swami's hermitage in India, Da Love-Ananda experienced a state of unqualified ecstasy, known as *nirvikalpa-samadhi*. He returned to India the following year, and during this second stay with Swami Muktananda he experienced a whole range of kundalini and visionary experiences, including the vision of the "blue pearl" that figures prominently in the teaching of the late Swami. All this was confirmed in a letter—a rare gesture for the Swami—that stated that Da Love-Ananda had "attained yogic liberation" and was now qualified to teach others.

But Da Love-Ananda knew that his spiritual journey had not yet come to an end. Nor had he any particular interest in teaching Kundalini Yoga. He felt certain that even the state of unqualified ecstasy he had repeatedly experienced, never mind any of the other visions and psychic phenomena, was dependent on the manipulation of the nervous system. Therefore it could not possibly be the same as enlightenment, or God-realization, which is continuous. So he intensified his practice of self-observation and surrender. Then on September 10, 1970, the following occurred:

> In an instant, I became profoundly and directly aware of what I am. It was a tacit realization, a direct knowledge in consciousness itself. It was consciousness itself without the addition of a communication from any other source . . . There was no thought involved in this. I am that Consciousness. There was no reaction either of joy or surprise. I am the One I recognized. I am that One . . . Then truly there was no more to realize. Every experience in my life had led to this. (1978c, pp. 134–135)

Subsequent to this awakening, Da Love-Ananda experienced a blossoming of spontaneous psychic activity, which continues to this day. It demonstrates his point that enlightenment is not the goal but the foundation of spiritual transformation.

Appendix 1

MICROMOTION OF THE BODY AS A FACTOR IN THE DEVELOPMENT OF THE NERVOUS SYSTEM

by Itzhak Bentov

Introduction

In the last few years, both young and old people in the United States and in Europe have taken up the practice of meditation. Regular practice of meditation has a calming and stabilizing effect on its practitioners (see Wallace and Benson 1972; Banquet 1972; Benson 1975). With prolonged practice, many physiological changes occur in the body. Among them is a change in the mode of functioning of the nervous system. These changes can be monitored by the application of a modified ballistocardiograph to a seated upright subject.

Theoretically, when meditation is practiced properly, a sequence of strong and unusual bodily reactions and unusual psychological states is eventually triggered. The "rising of the kundalini," as described in the classical literature of Yoga, is a stimulus or "energy" activating a "center," or chakra, at the base of the spine and working its way up the spine. The stimulus stops at several centers along the spine, as it rises. These centers are located opposite the major nerve plexuses in the abdomen and in the thorax, which are also stimulated in the process. Eventually the stimulus ends up in the head. Along its path, it often causes violent motion in some parts of the body, signifying that there is "resistance" to its passage. The rising of the kundalini may happen suddenly or over a period of several years. After entering the head, the stimulus continues down the face into the larynx and the abdominal cavity.

Most meditators realize that these reactions are caused by meditation and do not become alarmed. However, sometimes this mechanism can be triggered in nonmeditators. Our observations indicate that exposure to certain mechanical vibrations, electromagnetic waves, or sounds may trigger this mechanism. It is the purpose of this article to bring this mechanism and some of its symptoms to the attention of the medical profession.

Summary

The ballistocardiogram of a sitting subject, who is capable of altering his or her state of consciousness at will, shows a rhythmic sine wave pattern when the subject is in a deep meditative state. This is attributed to the development of a standing wave in the aorta, which is reflected in the rhythmic motion of the body. This resonating oscillator (the heart-aorta system) will rhythm entrain four additional oscillators, eventually resulting in a fluctuating magnetic field around the head.

Our initial experiments indicate that the five resonating systems are as follows:

1. The heart-aorta system produces an oscillation of about 7 Hz in the skeleton, including the skull. The upper part of the body also has a resonant frequency of about 7 Hz.

2. The skull accelerates the brain up and down, producing acoustical plane waves reverberating through the brain at KHz frequencies.

3. These acoustical plane waves are focused by the skull onto the ventricles, thus activating and driving standing waves within the third and lateral ventricles.

4. Standing waves within the cerebral ventricles in the audio and supersonic ranges stimulate the sensory cortex mechanically, resulting eventually in a stimulus traveling in a closed loop around each hemisphere. Such a traveling stimulus may be viewed as a "current."

5. As a result of these circular "currents," each hemisphere produces a pulsating magnetic field. These fields are of opposing polarities.

This magnetic field—radiated by the head acting as an antenna—interacts with the electric and magnetic fields already in the environment. We may consider the head as simultaneously a transmitting and receiving antenna, tuned to a particular one of the several resonant frequencies of the brain. Environmental fields may thus be fed back to the brain, thereby modulating that resonant frequency. The brain will interpret this modulation as useful information.

This paper presents a preliminary report on the possible mechanism of the so-called "kundalini." The kundalini effect is viewed by the author as part of the development of the nervous system. This development can be elicited by the practice of any of several different types of meditative techniques, or it may develop spontaneously. Research into this area is continuing, and investigation of the kundalini effect by different methods is in progress.

Micromotion Measurement with the Capacitive Probe

Small body motions accompanying the motion of blood through the circulatory system may be measured with a capacitive probe apparatus. A subject sits on a chair between two metal plates, one above the head, and one under the seat, 5 to 10 cm from the body.

The two plates of the capacitor are part of a tuned circuit. The movement of the subject will modulate the field between the two plates. This signal is processed and fed into a single channel recorder, which registers both the motion of the chest due to respiration and the movement of the body reacting to the motion of the blood in the heart-aorta system. The resulting recording trace (see Figure 2) is very similar to that of a ballistocardiogram (see Weissler 1974), in which the subject lies on a platform, to which are attached three mutually perpendicular accelerometers or strain gauges to measure the body's motion in response to blood flow. But in the capacitive probe measurements, gravitational forces and the elasticity of the skeleton and the general body build play important roles.

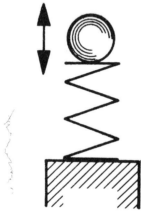

FIGURE 1: Mass on a spring.

As an analogy, a seated subject can be represented by a mass on a spring (see Figure 1): The spring is the spinal column and the mass is the weight of the upper part of the body. Upon the ejection of blood from the heart, this mass is set into motion and starts oscillating at its natural frequency when the person is in a deep meditative state.

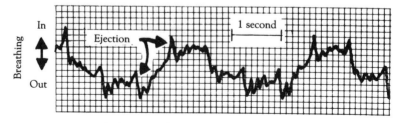

FIGURE 2: Baseline resting state record.

Figure 2 shows a baseline resting state record, in which the micromotion of the body is superimposed over the motion of the chest caused by breathing. These are the large slow waves of about a 3-second period, or 20 breaths/minute. The first 7-Hz wave is caused by the ejection of blood from the left ventricle, which makes the body recoil downward and sets the body oscillating. The second wave corresponds closely to the action of the blood flowing through the aortic arch, lifting the body up. The third wave occurs at about the same time as the closing of the aortic valve and the slight backflow of the blood, called the dichrotic notch. The first and third waves correspond closely to the first and second heart sounds.

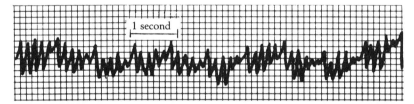

FIGURE 3: Deep meditative state record.

Figure 3 shows a recording in which the subject is in a deep meditative state, a few minutes after the baseline reading. Breathing is very shallow, as shown by the practically even level of the 7.5-Hz waves. The irregularity that characterized the baseline behavior (see Figure 2) is gone. Large amplitude regular waves—practically pure sine waves—are present. An almost pure sine wave is what characterizes this state. The body moves in a simple harmonic motion.

Figure 4 shows the return to baseline of the same subject.

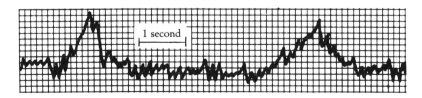

FIGURE 4: Return to baseline resting state record.

Breathing is deeper again; the irregularity of the wave pattern is back, but is not as irregular as before. Total elapsed time for the recording was about 20 minutes.

We have noticed that the regularity in rhythm is obtained at the expense of breathing. The subject can stay in the shallow breathing state for a long time without having to compensate later by deep rapid breathing. This is a state in which the body's demand for oxygen seems to be lowered. If one stops breathing for a while without being in a deep meditative state (see Wallace and Benson 1972), the same regular pattern will be achieved. However, oxygen deficiency builds up quickly and overbreathing will be necessary to restore balance, whereas in the meditative state this overbreathing does not occur.

The Development of a Standing Wave in the Aorta

The regular movement of the body indicates that a standing wave is set up in the vascular system, specifically in the aorta (see Bergel 1972). This is the only feasible explanation of the regular sine-wavelike behavior of the body. This standing wave, as will be shown later, has far-reaching consequences and affects several other resonant systems in the body, which are all driven by this large signal.

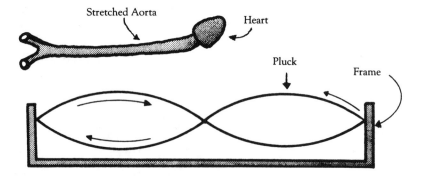

FIGURE 5: Comparison of the aorta to a stretched vibrating string. The length of the stretched aorta is equal to one half the wave length of the string.

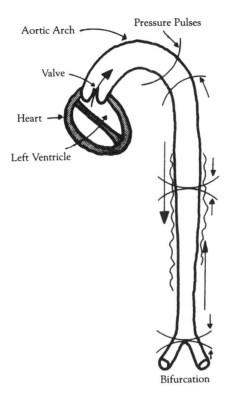

Aortic Arch

Pressure Pulses

Valve

Heart

Left Ventricle

Bifurcation

FIGURE 6: Collision of the oppositely traveling pressure pulses causes a destructive interference pattern and vibration of aortic walls.

The aorta is the major artery of the body. When the left ventricle of the heart ejects blood, the aorta, being elastic, balloons out just distal to the ventricle. Under these conditions, a pressure pulse travels down along the aorta. When the pressure pulse reaches the iliac bifurcation, part of it rebounds and starts traveling up the aorta (see Figures 5 and 6). When the timing of the pressure pulses traveling down the aorta coincides or is in phase with the reflected pressure pulses, a standing wave is achieved. This standing wave of approximately 7 Hz will cause the body to move in a rhythmic fashion, provided the aorta is properly tuned. Presumably, a feedback loop is set up between the bifurcation and the heart, which then regulates the breathing so as to make the lungs and the diaphragm contact the aorta and regulate its impedance. This allows the pressure pulse to be in phase with both the ejection and the dichrotic notch. This is an entirely automatic process during deep meditation.

Acoustical Plane Waves in the Body

The movement of the body is relatively small, 0.003 to 0.009 mm, but the body and particularly the head are very dense, tight structures. By moving up and down, the skull accelerates the brain with a mild impact in both directions (see Figure 7). This sets up acoustical and possibly electrical plane waves reverberating within the skull. The brain may be considered as a piezoelectric gel, converting mechanical vibrations into electrical vibrations, and conversely.

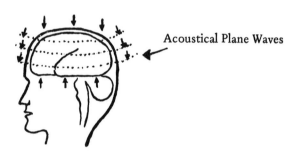

FIGURE 7: Acoustical plane waves moving through the brain.

The acoustical plane waves reflected from the cranial vault are focused upon the third and lateral ventricles of the brain, as shown in Figures 8 and 9 (see Ruch and Patton 1962). High-frequency acoustical waves generated by the heart are also reflected from the cranial vault and focused upon the third and lateral ventricles.

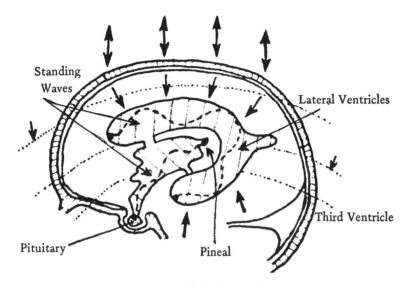

FIGURE 8: Lateral cross section of the brain, showing acoustical standing waves.

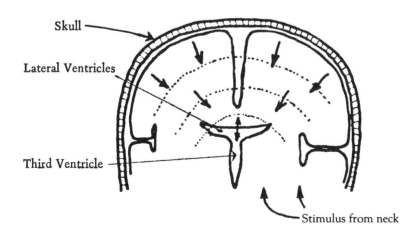

FIGURE 9: Frontal cross section of the brain.

Acoustical Standing Waves in the Ventricles

A hierarchy of frequencies couples the 7-Hz body movement to the higher frequencies in the ventricles.

The body can be considered as a bag of elastic skin containing stiff gel and supported by a rigid armature. The motion of the heart-aorta system sets this gel vibrating in different modes. Assuming the velocity of signal propagation to be 1,200m/sec, the fundamental frequencies for the different parts of the body would be along the vertical axis of the body: (1) the brain, 4,000 Hz; (2) circumference of the skull, 2,250 Hz; (3) the whole body length, 375 Hz; (4) the trunk and head, 750 Hz; (5) heart sounds, 35 to 2,000 Hz (see Stapp 1961). The high-frequency component of the heart sounds, although very low in intensity, may be able to drive the ventricles directly. The stimulus will be conducted by the left side of the neck, up into the skull, and reflected back from the cranial vault to the ventricles.

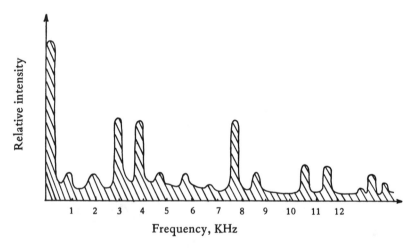

FIGURE 10: Frequency distribution of "inner sounds" heard by meditators.

Frequency distribution measurements of "inner sounds" reported by 156 meditators were made by asking each meditator to compare the sounds heard during meditation with sounds produced by an audio-frequency oscillator through an earphone in one ear. The subject rotated the oscillator frequency control to match oscillator tones with those heard or remembered as the "inner sound." The frequency distribution is not smooth, but shows several sharp peaks, harmonics of the fundamental frequency, and possibly beat frequencies produced between the third and lateral ventricles of the brain, which are connected by a fluid bridge. In the frequency range below 1 KHz, acoustical standing waves running through the entire body appear, as do the higher harmonics of the heartbeat and the heart sounds.

The Circular Sensory Cortex "Current"

Figure 11 shows a lateral or side view of the brain. A cross section of the left hemisphere, along line AB through the sensory cortex, is shown as Figure 12 (see Ruch and Patton 1962). The labels in Figure 12 show sensory cortex areas corresponding to specific

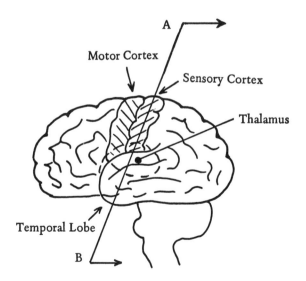

FIGURE 11: Lateral view of the brain, with section line AB.

sensory functions and to three pleasure centers that elicit pleasurable sensations when stimulated. These are: (1) the cingulate gyrus, (2) the lateral hypothalamus, and (3) the hippocampus and amygdala areas.

Just above the roof of the lateral ventricle starts the medial fissure, the cleft that separates the two hemispheres.

When a standing wave is present in the ventricles, the roof of the lateral ventricles acts as a taut skin on a drum that moves rapidly up and down, as shown in Figure 9.

The roof of the lateral ventricles is the corpus callosum, a bundle of nerve fibers connecting the two hemispheres (see Ruch and Patton 1962). The vibration of the corpus callosum and of the brain mass in general may serve as a pacesetter in the phase synchronization that occurs between the two hemispheres during meditation (see Banquet 1972).

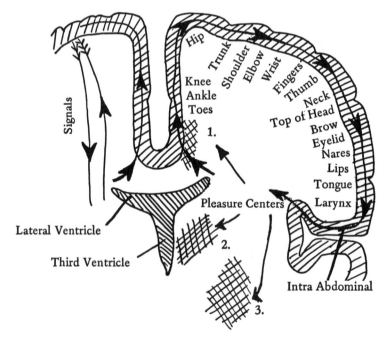

FIGURE 12: Cross section of the left hemisphere of the brain, through section line AB of Figure 11.

When the sensory cortex is stimulated electrically or mechanically, paresthesias occur in the area of the body corresponding to certain points on the cortex. These points are mapped out on the surface of the cortex as shown in Figure 12.

As the roof of the lateral ventricles vibrates, it stimulates first the toes, then the ankles, then the calves and thighs, and, as the stimulus rounds the corner of the hemisphere, the pelvis is stimulated. As the stimulus spreads along the cortex, it will affect the trunk, moving along the spine toward the head.

The cortex has different acoustical properties from the white matter and the cerebrospinal fluid. The white matter consists mostly of myelinated fibers, a fatty substance that will tend to damp out an acoustical signal. The cortex may be viewed as a water-based gel that conducts vibration well.

Thus, an acoustical interface exists between the white matter, the cortex, and the cerebrospinal fluid. The cortex will therefore preferentially tunnel the acoustical signal.

This mechanical vibratory action is assumed to cause electrical polarization of the tissue of the cortex, to allow enhanced conductivity of the tissue to the stimulus moving along the cortex. This moving stimulus may be viewed as a current. According to our hypothesis, this current is responsible for the effects of the "awakened kundalini" on the body (see Bucke 1970; Krishna 1974).

Sensory signals usually come to the cortex through the thalamus and go back the same way (see Figures 11 and 12). It is interesting to note that those parts of the body which are represented on the surface of the cortex facing the cranium are felt more strongly by a person experiencing the kundalini stimulus. Those chakras, or energy centers, are most actively felt, while portions of the cortex which are cushioned and are located inside the folds of the brain are less noticeable to the individual. This may well occur because the arch between the tops of the two hemispheres and the temporal areas are exposed to a double stimulus—one coming up from the ventricles and one coming down from the cranial vault, accelerating the brain downward. The larynx is the last point on the cortex facing the skull, and it is also the last chakra to be activated and strongly felt. Presumably, the stimulus continues inside the fold of the temporal lobe and closes the circuit, as shown in Figure 13.

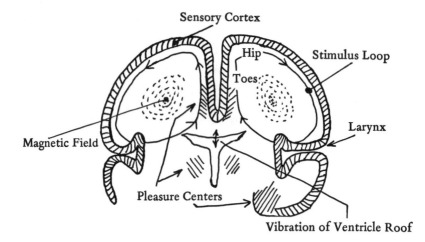

FIGURE 13: Frontal cross section of the brain.

This is shown by EEG measurements, indicating that during meditation there are currents of opposing polarity, relative to the midline, flowing along the sensory cortex of both hemispheres. These occur in both the alpha and theta range of brain wave frequencies.

As the stimulus travels through, it crosses an area that contains a pleasure center. When the pleasure center is thus stimulated, the meditator experiences a state of ecstasy. To reach that state it may take years of systematic meditation, or again, in certain people it may happen spontaneously.

As long as the four oscillators—the aorta, the heart sounds, the standing waves in the ventricles, and the circulating sensory stimulus or kundalini current—are in phase and resonating, all parts of the body move in harmony. The fifth oscillating circuit is activated when the sensory cortex tissue has been finally polarized to the point where there is a circulation of electrical current in the hemispheres and a magnetic field develops inside the core of each current ring, as shown in Figures 14 and 15 (see Cohen 1972).

This magnetic field pulsates in harmony with the other oscillators. The observed "normal" rate of the circulation of the sensory current is about 7 cycles/sec.

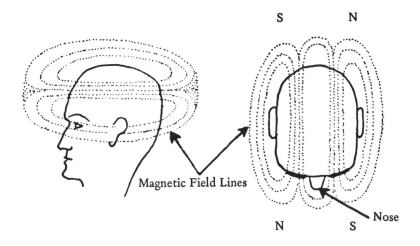

FIGURE 14: Lateral and top views of the head, showing magnetic field lines.

Pulsating magnetic fields of the order of 10^{-9} gauss are produced by the currents circulating in the brain. These currents may be detected by an electroencephalograph electrode on the skin surface of the head. However, they are quite variable (see Cohen 1972). The sensory cortex currents will produce fields of symmetrical shape but with polarities associated with the two brain hemispheres opposing each other, as shown in Figures 14 and 15.

Thus by meditating in a quiet sitting position, we slowly activate five tuned oscillators. One by one these oscillators are locked into rhythm. This results eventually in the development of a pulsating magnetic field around the head. When this occurs, one may simultaneously observe other characteristic and automatic changes in the functioning of the nervous and circulatory systems. It is the purpose of meditation to bring about these changes in order to increase the ability of the nervous system to handle stress and overcome it more easily. The noise level in the nervous system is thus reduced, and the system becomes more efficient and permits a fuller development of the person's latent physical and mental capacities.

Any of the five tuned oscillators can be triggered individually after a short period of stimulation. Any one of them will get the sensory cortex current circulating and will soon lock the heart and the body's motion into an artificial state of meditation. This is a dangerous practice, which may be traumatic to an inexperienced meditator.

Magnetic Feedback

Fifteen subjects sitting upright were subjected to hemispheric stimulation by an externally applied varying unipolar magnetic field of 0.5-gauss maximum intensity measured at the skin surface. The field was produced by a C-shaped electromagnet, with 30-cm pole gap spacing, activated by a voltage-offset sine wave power source, with a frequency of 3.75 Hz, and a stimulus duration of 2 minutes for each subject. The apparatus formed a closed magnetic circuit with lines of force going through the brain. The polarity of the applied field could be reversed. The responses of the subjects in a blind experiment were collected in tabular form (see Table 1).

Subject	Pushed & pulled by field	pain & press. in head	press-ure in eyes	Stimula-tion in back of head	Pulse felt in neck	High-pitched sound in head	Press-ure in ears	Meditates
1	+				+			−
2		+				+		+
3		+	+		+			+
4			+		+			−
5	+							−
6	+							+
7	+	+	+					−
8		+	+	+				+
9						+	+	−
10	+							+
11		+						+
12	+	+		+	+			+
13		+		+	+	+		−
14	+							+
15	+	+						+
	8	8	4	3	5	3	1	

TABLE 1: Summary of responses of 15 subjects to unipolar 3.75-Hz, 0.5-gauss maximum intensity, 2-minute duration magnetic field stimulation applied to one hemisphere of the brain.

More than 50 percent of the subjects tested described sensations of pain or pressure in the head, also a sensation of being pushed and pulled by the applied magnetic field. These results suggest an interaction of the field around the head with the externally applied field.

Discussion

The symptom-sign of this "sensory-motor cortex syndrome," or what has been characterized as the kundalini process in ancient literature, can be quite variable and sporadic. Its complete presentation usually begins as a transient paresthesia of the toes or ankle with numbness and tingling. Occasionally, there is diminished sensitivity to touch or pain, or even partial paralysis of the foot or leg. The process most frequently begins on the left side and ascends in a sequential manner from foot to leg to hip, to involve completely the left side of the body, including the face. Once the hip is involved, it is not uncommon to experience an intermittent throbbing or rhythmic rumblinglike sensation in the lower lumbar and sacral spine. This is followed by an ascending sensation that rises along the spine to the cervical and occipital regions of the head.

At these latter areas, severe pressure-caused occipital headaches and cervical neck aches may be experienced at times. These pressures, usually transient but occasionally persistent, may also be felt anywhere along the spine, right or left side of the chest, or different parts of the head and the eyes. Some individuals will notice tingling sensations descending along the face to the laryngeal areas. The tracheolaryngeal region may also be felt as a sudden rushing of air to and fro. Respiration may become spasmodic with involuntarily occurring maximum expirations. Various auditory tones have been noted, from constant low-pitched hums to high-pitched ringing. Visual aberrations and a temporary decrease or loss of vision has been observed. The sequence of symptoms continues later, down into the lower abdominal region.

Because a particular symptom or sign of the altered sensory and motor systems may occur or persist for months or years, the sequence of symptoms may not be obvious, nor appear causally connected. Also, only in a few of the known cases will all of the symptoms in this sequence become vividly apparent to each person. Normally, physical and laboratory examination reveals either little or no pathology and therefore, except in rare cases, many of the complaints are probably dismissed as psychosomatic or neurotic symptoms.

Meditation has been considered, here and elsewhere, as a stress removal process (see Selye 1956; Benson 1975). The symptoms noted above are indications that release of stress is taking place. Stress, as defined by Hans Selye (1956), is a "state manifested by a specific syndrome which consists of all the nonspecifically induced changes within a biological system." The intensity of the symptoms is an index of the severity of the stress being released. On the whole, these symptoms should be looked upon as a positive sign of normalization of the body. The unusual aspect of this mechanism is that the release of stress is experienced as a localized stimulation of a particular part of the body, as opposed to the accepted notion that stress is a diffuse general state.

A large percentage of individuals who meditate and who have previously used psychedelic drugs for extended periods of time, or are experiencing unusual stress, are more likely to show these symptoms. These will eventually subside by themselves, without the need for any medical intervention.

It is the spontaneously triggered cases that present a problem, since the individual does not know the cause of these symptoms, and tends to panic. The psychological problems may mimic schizophrenia, and be diagnosed as such by the physician. As a consequence, drastic procedures may be used to alleviate the problem.

An awareness of the existence of the above-noted symptoms and the mechanism triggering them is important, especially in view of the constantly increasing number of persons practicing meditation, who are therefore likely to experience these effects of stress release.

Possible Rhythm Entrainment Effects

Our experiments show that when a person in deep meditation is suddenly called to come out and stop meditating, the normal response is reluctance to abandon that state and a lapsing back into deep meditation repeatedly. This seems to suggest that a "locking in" situation is present. It is well known that the larger the number of frequency-locked oscillators in a system, the more stable the system and the more difficult it is to disturb.

When a situation exists where there are two oscillators vibrating at frequencies close to each other, the oscillator operating at a higher frequency will usually lock into step the slower oscillator. This is rhythm entrainment. When, in the state of deep meditation, a person goes into sine wave oscillation at approximately 7 cycles/sec, there is a tendency for him or her to be locked into the frequency of the planet (see Figure 16).

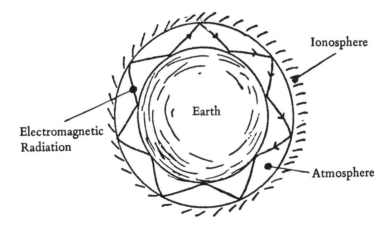

FIGURE 16: The earth's atmosphere is shown as a resonant cavity.

We have talked about resonant cavities and how a stimulus can set such a cavity vibrating at its own resonant frequency. Our planet has a conductive layer around it called the ionosphere, which starts about 80 km from the earth's surface. The cavity between the earth and the ionosphere (the atmosphere) is also a resonant cavity.

Certain types of electromagnetic radiation travel through this cavity, being reflected alternately between the earth's surface and the ionosphere, and vibrate at characteristic resonant frequencies.

In 1957 W. O. Schumann calculated the earth-ionosphere cavity resonance frequencies at 10.6, 18.3, and 25.9 Hz. More recent work by J. Toomey and C. Polk (1970) gave the values 7.8, 14.1, 26.4, and 32.5 Hz. The lowest frequency, 7.8 Hz, is approximately equal to the velocity of electromagnetic radiation divided by the earth's circumference:

$$\frac{2.998 \times 10^8 \text{ m/sec}}{4.003 \times 10^7 \text{ m}} = 7.489 \text{ or } 7.5 \text{ Hz}$$

This is the reciprocal of the time required for a beam of electromagnetic radiation to go around the earth.

Our planet is very much affected by the sun and quite closely coupled to its plasma fields. These two bodies and their interacting fields form our immediate environment. The sun produces energy in a wide spectrum, from powerful X-rays to acoustical signals (see Ewing 1967; Thomsen 1968). The solar wind shapes the magnetosphere and the plasmaspheres of our planet. All these layers contain charged particles produced by the sun. In the Van Allen belt, these particles oscillate back and forth along the magnetic lines of the earth between the north and the south poles. Much of this vibration occurs in the frequency range of 1 to 40 Hz, well within physiological frequencies (see Konig 1971).

There is a strong coupling between these oscillations and the changes in the magnetic field of the earth. These microfluctuations of the magnetic field are on the order of 10^{-5} gauss, about 10,000 times stronger than the fields around our heads. We live within this constantly active natural electromagnetic environment, with the added perturbations of broadcasting television and radio stations (see Becker 1972).

Given these conditions, it would be reasonable to assume that the fluctuations in these planetary environmental fields have affected human evolution in subtle ways over the ages—in ways that are not quite clear to us yet.

Our knowledge of physiology considers the present state of the human nervous system as being at the peak of its development. However, the present discussion suggests a mechanism that may cause changes in the cerebrospinal system. When a fetus develops in the womb, it undergoes changes that mirror human evolution from a fish through the amphibian to the mammal. But our findings suggest that this evolution very probably has not come to a halt with the way our nervous system is functioning at present. The hidden potential of our nervous system may be vast.

The mechanism outlined above describes a possible next step in the evolution of the nervous system, which can be accelerated by the use of certain techniques. We can speculate that this development will have the effect of an increased awareness of the self as a part of a much larger system. We can postulate that our magnetic "antennae" will bring in information about our extended system—the earth and the sun—and will allow us to interpret geophysical phenomena and signals to better advantage.

In this connection the work of Walcott and Green (1974) is of particular interest, since it shows that one of the orientation mechanisms of the homing pigeon depends on the magnetic fields of the earth. Indications are that the pigeon's built-in magnetic field is interacting with the earth's magnetic field. The pigeon's field would be analogous to the magnetic field around our head, when intensified by the sensory cortex "current."

Acknowledgments

The author thanks Earl Ettienne, Ph.D., of Harvard Medical School, Richard P. Ingrasci, M.D., of Boston State Hospital, and William A. Tiller, Ph.D., of Stanford University, for their help in reviewing this report and for many valuable suggestions.

Special thanks are due to Paul Nardella of Easton, Massachusetts, for his design and construction of the electronic equipment used in making the measurements described in this report.

References

Banquet, J. 1972. "Electroencephalography and Clinical Neurophysiology." *EEG and Meditation* 33:454.

Becker, R. 1972. "Electromagnetic Forces and Life Processes." *M. I. T. Technology Review* 75, no. 2 (December):32.

Benson, H. 1975. *The Relaxation Response.* New York: Wm. Morrow.

Bergel, D. 1972. *Cardio-Vascular Fluid Dynamics.* New York: Academic Press. Chapter 10.

Bucke, R. 1970. *Cosmic Consciousness.* New York: E. P. Dutton.

Cohen, D. 1972. "Magnetoencephalograph: Detection of the Brain's Electrical Activity with a Superconducting Magnetometer." *Science* 175, no. 4022 (February 11):664–666.

Ewing, A. 1967. "The Noisy Sun: Ion Signals Across Space." *Science News* 92, no. 11 (September 9):250.

Gauquelin, M. 1974. *The Cosmic Clocks.* New York: Avon Books.

Konig, H. 1971. "Biological Effects of Low Frequency Electrical Phenomena," *Interdisciplinary Cycle Research* 2, no. 3.

Krishna, G. 1974. *Higher Consciousness.* New York: Julian Press.

Luisada, A. 1972. *The Sounds of the Normal Heart.* St. Louis: Warren H. Green Publishing Co.

New, P. "Arterial Stationary Waves." *American Journal of Roentgenology* 97, no. 2:488–499.

Persinger, M., ed. 1974. *ELF and VLF Electromagnetic Field Effects.* New York: Plenum Press.

Ruch, T., H. Patton, J. Woodbury, and A. Towe. 1962. *Neurophysiology.* Philadelphia: Saunders Publishing Co.

Schumann, W. 1957. "Elektrische Eigenschwingungen des Hohlraumes Erde-Luft-Ionosphäre." *Zeitschrift für Angewandte Physik* 9:373–378.

Selye, H. 1956. *The Stress of Life.* New York: McGraw-Hill.

Stapp, J. P. 1961. "The 'G' Spectrum in Space Flight Dynamics." *Lectures in Aerospace Medicine* (January 16–20).

Tart, C. 1969. *Altered States of Consciousness.* New York: John Wiley.

Thomsen, D. 1968. "On the Edge of Space." *Science News* 94, no. 9 (August 31):216.

Walcott, C., and R. Green. 1974. "Orientation of Homing Pigeons Altered by a Change in the Direction of an Applied Magnetic Field." *Science* 184, no. 4133 (April 12).

Wallace, K., and H. Benson. 1972. "The Physiology of Meditation." *Scientific American* (February).

Weissler, A. 1974. *Non-Invasive Cardiology.* New York: Grune & Stratton. Chapter on ballistocardiography.

Appendix 2

THE GOD-INTOXICATED
MASTS OF INDIA

"Masts"—from Hindi *mast*, meaning "head, skull"—is the name used by the Indian adept Meher Baba to refer to "God-intoxicated" men and women. From a conventional point of view, they are "not right in their heads" or "out of their minds." But they can also be looked upon as "mutations" toward a primal link with the transcendental Reality. These Masts are thought to arise in times of crisis to fulfill certain vital functions for the benefit of all humanity.

Because of the strangeness of their behavior they may easily be mistaken for psychotics. However, their condition may be distinguished from schizophrenia by their compelling attractiveness to the ordinary folk who gather around to serve and be near them, and a recognition of them as saints by their followers. They have an obvious lack of interest in dealing with ordinary life situations, their own physical needs, emotional relationships, or even intellectual functioning in the ordinary sense. Meher Baba worked with both Masts and psychotics, and he carefully distinguished between the two. He made no effort to cure them. His labors with them were never explained by him and must remain obscure.

The Masts seem to appear only within a solid religious tradition. W. Donkin (1948), the physician who accompanied Meher Baba for years, believed that they were pivotal points of spiritual intervention: forces around which, and through whom, other spiritual influences could work to serve humanity. Their power seemed to him more autonomous and primal than that of the mind or heart of other saintly persons.

The kundalini process at times evokes feelings and behavior similar to those of the Masts of India. In fact, the Masts' peculiar condition may well be the result of spontaneous kundalini activity.

The question poses itself: What would we in the West do with such folk? The answer is not far to seek, for we would surely have these gentle saints referred to our clinics and asylums. What a tremendous loss this would be!

Appendix 3

SENSITIVITY IN
THE HUMAN ORGANISM

The basis for all creativity is sensitivity of the physical organism. Providing no negative events intervene, this capacity is developed on a regular schedule of unfolding, from infancy to adulthood. In due course, as we leave the sheltering environment of our early home life, this growing sensitivity brings us in tune wtih the great world outside. Ideally we also contact our own inner reality and processes so that our responsiveness becomes self-aware—not only instinctively tuned in, but also firmly rooted in mature understanding.

Conceptual responsiveness should properly be a later addition, though it must never become a substitute for instinctive ways of being in touch with the world around us. The instinctive harmony is our natural animal heritage. It can be seen in the remarkable ability of dogs and horses to sense the needs or whereabouts of their trainers even when the latter are far distant. Moreover, many animals are now known to prepare in advance for floods, earthquakes, and other natural disasters, which commonly catch people today by surprise. In Appendix 1, Bentov has suggested that magnetic fields around the head, generated by the effects of the kundalini, could enable a human being to orient himself or herself to planetary and solar electromagnetic fluctuations in a way similar to that achieved by pigeons and other migratory birds.

In my studies I have observed the development of these

instinctive and—on a higher, self-aware level—intuitive powers as a difficult and painful rebirth occurring later in life, and even then only in rare individuals. But in certain primitive tribes such as the Bushmen and Australian aborigines, these abilities unfold easily and naturally from childhood on. Why should we in the West need two births to claim our natural birthright? The instinctive-intuitive mechanism must be revived because it has in the meantime "died"—or, to put it bluntly, it has been killed.

Genetic inheritance is not alone instrumental in the development of this sensitivity. Negative environmental factors must also be taken into account. In the West, for instance, factors encountered before birth and continuously thereafter act to curtail the growth of human feeling (see Pearce 1976). In the sensitive human organism, with proper protection of the psyche in its early development, the kundalini cycle begins easily and normally. But against the background of inherent weaknesses and with negative environmental factors present, the organism becomes overwhelmed.

Each system and function probably has its own natural time to become activated and grow at a pace determined from within to ensure the harmonious development of the whole child. But our Western culture cuts off the tender shoots of the delicate plant of feeling with the cold sharpness of mechanical insensitivity, while otherwise force-feeding vitamins and other stimulants to the barely sprouted seedling of conceptual thought. In this way, the entire system is thrown out of balance, and harmonious development becomes impossible. (Joseph Chilton Pearce, for instance, has suggested that children should not be taught to read until the age of ten.)

In some people, the result is schizophrenia, which is a basic breakdown in the processes of thought and feeling. In those who are more resilient, armoring occurs and they may become depressed. They lose touch with their emotional world, and show a hardening of the heart, becoming tough and relatively unresponsive to both outer and inner worlds. At last they succumb to emotional petrification and senility.

Vestiges of the feeling process are detectable in the theta-delta activity of the brain waves, which, though normally subdued in the waking state, are seen in certain sleep stages. Thus the feeling or intuitive capacity can be curtailed in our conscious self, but we can never extinguish it in the subconscious realm.

If death in the feeling dimension is brought about in part by the stress of emotional insensitivity and premature conceptualization enforced on the young child by a mechanized environment, how can its rebirth possibly be effected in later life?

One way to increase one's responsiveness to the inner and outer environment is by fasting. This predictably enhances the senses of touch, smell, taste, hearing, and vision. There is also an increased sensitivity to internal stimuli, which is shown by the greater incidence of visionary or auditory experiences.

Fasting in the normal or even in the schizophrenic state adds stress to the organism. This physiological crisis, similar to an external crisis, brings the organism back to its senses. The impact of reality becomes more tangible and immediate, hence more success-ful in moving the organism toward behavior that is consonant with its new view of reality.

Stress, in general, prepares the individual to see reality for what it is, and puts the biological organism in a state of readiness, or physical and mental alertness, to meet the emergency situation and to survive. In other words, it is stress that is necessary later in life to shock the organism into a return to the feeling self, which was overwhelmed by excessive stress early in life. The conceptual mechanism at that developmental stage was better able than the still undeveloped feeling mechanism to deal with the interpersonal crises of infancy. Yet, in the end, the organism has to return to the feeling system in order to cope with the more basic needs of the kind of biological crisis that is provoked by fasting, war, or other life-and-death situations.

The kundalini process is a process of physiological sensitization that can attune us to our inner and outer environments. Its effectiveness is, however, largely determined by the degree to which the individual has reawakened to the feeling dimension of his or her life. Only then can the kundalini experience be integrated.

Appendix 4

NOTE FOR PHYSICIANS AND NEUROLOGISTS

There are a number of medical disorders that may develop some of the symptoms of the complex discussed in this book. These generally are no problem for a well-trained diagnostician. However, the three young women who saw neurologists had symptoms that were converted to more serious manifestations because of their ignorance and fear, augmented by some perplexity on the part of their physicians. It is not feasible in this book to discuss the many neurological disorders that could be considered. Instead, I will use one rather obscure disorder as a model for the whole class that displays motor, sensory, and febrile changes that may appear in the kundalini complex as well.

Icelandic Disease

Icelandic disease (see Roueche 1965) is probably of viral nature, has an acute onset characterized by pains in the neck and back, paresthesias and hyperesthesias (extremes of skin sensitivity), muscle weakness (as in polio), paresis, nervousness, insomnia, loss of memory, and terrifying dreams. Those struck are usually persons in their twenties and thirties. It is never fatal. Some of the cases show pain in arms, legs, and back, as well as headaches. There may also be delirium during the day, sensations of imbalance, and strange feelings in the legs. Some patients report tingling and sweating in the hands and feet, ringing in the ears, and confusion. All these symptoms may be noted in our physio-kundalini cases.

The victims are more often women than men, and the epidemics tend to strike members of isolated or closed communities. Occasionally the emotional overlay of tension, anxiety, and depression is quite marked. The disorder has a prolonged and relapsing course which may last for a year or more. It is notable that none of the areas of paresthesias correspond to any recognized area of innervation.

The specialists (see Roueche 1965) in these cases were so confused by this array of signs and symptoms that the "bughouse possibility actually occurred to us . . . the more of their complaints we heard the more we began to wonder about a functional (neurotic) explanation" (p. 216).

One of the patients even experienced internal vibrations as if she was shaking all over inside. This is a common symptom in our kundalini cases.

This disorder has received several names. Among the most familiar are Icelandic disease, acute infective encephalomyelitis, atypical poliomyelitis, and epidemic neuromyasthenia. I have seen one case of this disorder in a meditator and thought seriously, for a time, that this young woman might be in the throes of the physio-kundalini complex.

The only symptom these cases do not report that is common in kundalini cases is the perception of internal light. However, these patients would have to be re-questioned to be sure that this symptom is actually missing. A physician would no more think of asking about such a possibility than a teacher of Yoga would consider measuring the temperature of the reported hot areas of his or her students' bodies.

Appendix 5

QUESTIONS FOR
RESEARCH PARTICIPANTS

The following questions have been formulated as a guide for physicians and researchers exploring the psychosislike states that may accompany physio-kundalini processes. I am particularly interested in detailed descriptions of pure sensory experiences rather than their interpretations.

If you wish to participate, please send your case history and any relevant information, including the place, date, and (if known) time of your birth, to the author at the following address: *175 Cascade Court, Rohnert Park, CA 94928.* Your account should include brief descriptions of any psychic experiences such as psychokinetic effects, clairvoyance, ESP, etc.

Please do not send original documents since I cannot guarantee the return of any materials. Your information will be treated confidentially, though I may wish to draw from it anonymously in a future edition of this book, unless you specifically ask me not to.

1. Do you hear sounds such as tones, music, hissing, roaring, thunder, drumming, or the sound of cymbals when no such sounds are produced outside your head? Do the sounds *seem* to come from inside or outside your head?

2. Do you have visualizations or visual hallucinations? Do you experience light inside your head or body, or see the environment as illuminated by other than normal means? What color are the

lights, how bright are they, and of what duration? Do they have a particular form?

3. Do you sense unusual heat or cold in your body or on your skin? Does it move from place to place or stay in one area? Is there any objective evidence of temperature change? In other words, can the heat be measured by a thermometer? If so, for how long at a time? How often do these temperature changes occur and how large are they?

4. Do you have sensations of tickling, tingling, vibrating, itching, crawling—pleasant or unpleasant—within the body or on the skin? Do these sensations move around in a patterned manner? Are the movements the same on both sides? Where do they start and to where do they move? Note especially if they start in the legs and move toward the back, neck, head, and face, in that order.

5. Do you experience spontaneous involuntary positioning of the limbs, fingers, or the whole body? Are there jerky, smooth, sinuous, rhythmic, spasmodic, or violent, involuntary body movements? Do you ever inadvertently cry out, grunt, yell, or scream? Do you ever stare into space for long periods of time or appear wild-eyed? Are there odd breathing patterns at times? If so, do these experiences occur most often when you are alone, sitting quietly, or while lying in bed?

BIBLIOGRAPHIC REFERENCES

Andrade, H., S. Hashizume, and G. Playfair. 1975. "Recurrent Patterns in RSPK Cases." *Second International Congress on Psychotronic Research*. Monte Carlo: International Association for Psychotronic Research.

Arundale, G. S. 1978. *Kundalini: An Occult Experience*. Adyar, India: Theosophical Publishing House. First published in 1938.

Avalon, A. [John Woodroffe]. 1974. *The Serpent Power*. New York: Dover Publications. First published in 1919.

Behari, B. 1971. *Sufis, Mystics and Yogis of India*. Bombay: Bharatiya Vidya Bhavan.

Bentov, I. 1977. *Stalking the Wild Pendulum*. New York: E. P. Dutton.

Berman, M. 1984. *The Reenchantment of the World*. New York: Bantam Books.

Blofeld, J. 1970. *The Tantric Mysticism of Tibet*. New York: E. P. Dutton.

Brenner, D., S. Williamson, and L. Kaufman. 1975. "Visually Evoked Magnetic Fields of the Human Brain." *Science* (October 31).

Brody, S., and S. Axelrod. 1970. *Anxiety and Ego Formation in Infancy*. New York: International Universities Press.

Bucke, R. 1970. *Cosmic Consciousness*. New York: E. P. Dutton.

Butterworth, E. A. S. 1970. *The Tree at the Navel of the Earth*. Berlin: Walter de Gruyter.

Campbell, J. 1974. *The Mythic Image*. Princeton: Princeton University Press.

Castaneda, C. 1968. *The Teachings of Don Juan*. New York: Ballantine Books.

Condon, W., and L. Sander. 1974. "Neonate Movement Is Synchronized with Adult Speech: Interactional Participation and Language Acquisition." *Science* (11 January):99–101.

Courtois, F. 1970. *An Experience of Enlightenment.* Tokyo: Shunju-Sha.

Cousens, G. 1986. *Spiritual Nutrition and The Rainbow Diet.* Boulder, Colo.: Cassandra Press.

Crookall, R. 1970. *The Study and Practice of Astral Projection.* London: Aquarian Press.

Da Free John [Da Love-Ananda]. 1978a. *The Enlightenment of the Whole Body.* Middletown, Calif.: Dawn Horse Press.

_____. 1978b. *The Method of the Siddhas.* Middletown, Calif.: Dawn Horse Press.

_____. 1978c. *The Knee of Listening.* Clearlake, Calif.: Dawn Horse Press.

_____. 1980. *Compulsory Dancing.* Clearlake, Calif.: Dawn Horse Press.

Dobrin, R., C. Kirsch, S. Kirsch, J. Pierrakos, E. Schwartz, T. Wolff, and Y. Zeira. 1975. "Experimental Measurements of the Human Energy Field." In S. Krippner and D. Rubin, eds., *The Energies of Consciousness.* New York: Gordon and Breach.

Donkin, W. 1948. *The Wayfarers.* Bombay: A. Irani.

Dossey, L. 1982. *Space, Time & Medicine.* Boulder, Colo.: Shambhala.

Durckheim, K. 1962. *Hara: The Vital Centre of Man.* London: Allen & Unwin.

Einstein, A. 1949. *The World As I See It.* New York: Philosophical Library.

Eliade, M. 1968. *Myths, Dreams and Mysteries.* London: Collins.

Feuerstein, G. 1980. *The Bhagavad-Gita: Yoga of Contemplation and Action.* New Delhi: Arnold-Heinemann.

Funderburk, J. 1977. *Science Studies Yoga: A Review of Physiological Data.* Honesdale, Pa.: Himalayan International Institute.

Gebser, J. 1985. *The Ever-Present Origin.* Athens, Ohio: Ohio University Press.

Goswami, S. S. 1980. *Layayoga: An Advanced Method of Concentration.* London: Routledge & Kegan Paul.

Greeley, A., and W. McCready. 1975. "Are We a Nation of Mystics?" *New York Times Magazine Section* (January 26).

Green, A. 1975. Paper presented at the Transpersonal Psychology Conference, Stanford University, July.

James, W. 1958. *The Varieties of Religious Experience.* New York: New American Library. First published in 1929.

Jonas, G. 1972. "Manfred Clynes and the Science of Sentics." *Saturday Review* (May 13).

Jung, C. G. 1964. *Civilization in Transition.* New York: Pantheon Books.

_____. 1975. "Psychological Commentary on Kundalini Yoga." *Spring.*

_____, and J. W. Hauer. 1932. "Kundalini Yoga." Unpublished manuscript.

Katz, R. 1973. "Education for Transcendence: Lessons from the !Kung Zhu Twasi." *Journal of Transpersonal Psychology* (No. 2).

_____. 1982. *Boiling Energy: Community Healing among the Kalahari Kung.* Cambridge, Mass.: Harvard University Press.

Krishna, G. 1971. *Kundalini: Evolutionary Energy in Man.* Berkeley: Shambhala.

_____. 1973. "The True Aim of Yoga." *Psychic* (January/February).

_____. 1975. "Science and Kundalini." Paper presented at the Seminar on Yoga, Science and Man, New Delhi.

Luk, C. 1973. *Taoist Yoga.* New York: Samuel Weiser.

Lu K'uan Yü [C. Luk]. 1972. *The Secrets of Chinese Meditation.* New York: Samuel Weiser.

MacIver, J. 1983. *The Glimpse.* Roslyn Heights, N.Y.: Libra Publishers.

Manning, M. 1975. *The Link.* New York: Holt, Rinehart & Winston.

Maslow, A. 1973. *The Farther Reaches of Human Nature.* Harmondsworth, England: Penguin Books.

Monroe, R. 1972. *Journeys Out of the Body.* London: Souvenir Press.

Morris, F. 1974. "Exorcising the Devil in California." *Fate* (July/August).

_____. 1975. *Self-Hypnosis in Two Days.* New York: E. P. Dutton.

Motoyama, H. 1981. *Theories of the Chakras: Bridge to Higher Consciousness.* Wheaton: Quest Books.

Muktananda, Swami. 1974. *The Play of Consciousness.* Campbell, Calif.: Shree Gurudev Ashram.

Muldoon, S. J. 1968. *The Projection of the Astral Body.* London: Rider.

—————. 1969. *The Phenomenon of Astral Projection.* London: Rider.

Mumford, L. 1954. *In the Name of Sanity.* New York: Harcourt, Brace and Company.

Narayanananda, Swami. 1960. *The Primal Power in Man.* Rishikesh, India: Prasad and Company.

Neumann, E. 1970. *The Origins and History of Consciousness.* Princeton: Princeton University Press.

Nikhilananda, Swami. 1942. *The Gospel of Sri Ramakrishna.* New York: Ramakrishna-Vivekananda Center.

Pearce, J. C. 1976. *The Magical Child.* New York: E. P. Dutton.

Pelletier, K. 1977. *Mind as Healer, Mind as Slayer.* New York: Dell Publishing.

Penfield, W. 1958. *The Excitable Cortex in Conscious Man.* Springfield, Ill.: Charles C. Tomas.

Prigogine, I., and I. Stengers. 1984. *Order Out of Chaos: Man's New Dialogue with Nature.* New York: Bantam Books.

Reich, C. A. 1971. *The Greening of America.* Harmondsworth, England: Penguin Books.

Rohrbach, P. 1963. *The Search For St. Thérèse.* New York: Dell.

Roszak, T. 1971. *The Making of a Counter Culture.* London: Faber and Faber.

Roueche, B. 1965. "Annals of Medicine in the Bughouse." *The New Yorker* (November 27):205–225.

Roy, D. K., and I. Devi. 1974. *Pilgrims of the Stars.* New York: Dell.

Sivananda Radha. 1978. *Kundalini: Yoga for the West.* Spokane, Wash.: Timeless Books.

Sivananda Saraswati, Swami. 1980. *Sure Ways to Self Realisation.* Monghyr, India: Sivanandashram.

Teilhard de Chardin, P. 1977. *The Future of Man*. London: Collins.

Thérèse of Lisieux. 1962. *Autobiography of St. Thérèse of Lisieux*. Translated by R. Knox. New York: P. J. Kenedy.

Tweedie, I. 1979. *The Chasm of Fire*. Tisbury, England: Element Books.

Underhill, E. 1961. *Mysticism*. New York: E. P. Dutton.

Vishnu Tirtha, Swami. 1962. *Devatma Shakti*. Rishikesh, India: Yoga Shri Peeth.

Walcott, C., and R. Green. 1974. "Orientation of Homing Pigeons Altered by a Change in the Direction of an Applied Magnetic Field." *Science* 184 (April 12):180–184.

Walker, B. 1982. *Tantrism: Its Secret Principles and Practices*. Wellingborough, England: Aquarian Press.

Walsh, R. 1984. "Journey Beyond Belief." *Journal of Humanistic Psychology* 24:30–65.

Wolfe, W. T. 1978. *And the Sun Is Up: Kundalini Rises in the West*. Red Hook, N.Y.: Academy Hill Press.

Woodroffe, J. 1929. *Mahamaya: The World as Power: Power as Consciousness (Chit-Shakti)*. Madras, India: Ganesh.

_____. 1978. *Shakti and Shakta*. New York: Dover Publications. First published in 1918.

Also available from Integral Publishing:

STRUCTURES OF CONSCIOUSNESS
THE GENIUS OF JEAN GEBSER
—AN INTRODUCTION AND CRITIQUE

by Georg Feuerstein

Quality paperback, 240 pages, with glossary, bibliography, and index
ISBN: 0-941255-20-4, $14.95 (Canada $18.95)

"**This is an important book introducing an important thinker. It is a contribution to both knowledge and wisdom. No mean feat in our time.**"
—Herbert D. Long, Th.D.
Former Dean, Harvard University

"**Feuerstein takes up where Ken Wilber leaves off. His book will be useful for those who intuit that heart and spirit are at the core of human consciousness.**"
—Fred Alan Wolf, Ph.D.
Author, *Star Wave, The Body Quantum*

What role does consciousness play in the present civilizational crisis? How is the history of consciousness alive in each person? What hidden configurations define the way we feel and think about reality? Who am I? Whence do I come? Whither do I go? How shall I live? Why must we participate in, rather than merely endure, today's great cultural transformation?

These are key questions for which the Swiss cultural philosopher Jean Gebser (1905–1973) has supplied ingenious and compelling answers. In *Structures of Consciousness*, Georg Feuerstein shows why Gebser's comprehensive work is one of our century's most important intellectual contributions to a new self-understanding and profound spiritual reorientation.

On the basis of Gebser's epochal work, Feuerstein offers a bold interpretation of the evolutionary unfolding of human consciousness from prehistoric times to the present age of uncertainty. His book introduces Jean Gebser as one of modern Europe's most sensitive, versatile, and daring philosopher-poets.

Central to Gebser's work is the proposition, first formulated by him in the 1930s, that today a new style of consciousness is trying to emerge. Gebser's careful documentation and penetrating analysis distinguish his work from the many "New Age" ideologies. In *Structures of Consciousness*, Feuerstein shows how Gebser's position is different and unique. At the same time, he challenges not only current approaches to the study of Gebserian thought but also aspects of Gebser's work itself.

This book is essential reading for anyone concerned with the Big Questions, whether professionally or not. It will be of particular interest to readers of authors like Pierre Teilhard de Chardin, Aurobindo Ghose, Carl Gustav Jung, Lewis Mumford, Guy Murchie, Ken Wilber, and Arthur Young.

From the Contents:

Jean Gebser—The Man and His Era
On the Nature of Consciousness and Reality
The Archaic Structure of Consciousness—The Garden of Eden
The Magical Structure of Consciousness—Pars Pro Toto
The Mythical Structure of Consciousness—I Feel, Therefore I Am
The Mental Structure of Consciousness—Man, the Measure of All Things
The Rational Consciousness—The Dominion of the Ego
The Emergent Consciousness—Transparent Self and World
The Spiritual Import of Gebser's Work
The Play of Consciousness in Daily Life
A Note on Gebser's Methodology

About Jean Gebser:

Jean Gebser started out as a poet and literary critic to become one of the wisest diagnosticians of our time. From the 1940s on he wrote and lectured about the positive significance of the far-reaching cultural changes witnessed after the turn of the century.

The English translation of his major work, *The Ever-Present Origin*, was published by Ohio University Press in 1986.

Jean Gebser was Professor of Comparative Civilizations at the University of Salzburg, Austria.

INDEX